THE

DRAMA OF CHRIST'S

COMING

THE

DRAMA OF CHRIST'S COMING

Wilfrid Harrington, O.P.

Michael Glazier, Inc.
Wilmington, Delaware

WILFRID HARRINGTON, O.P., a graduate of the University of St. Thomas, Rome, and École Biblique, Jerusalem, is Professor of Scripture at the Milltown Institute of Theology and Philosophy and the Dominican House of Studies, Dublin. He has lectured in the U.S.A. and Great Britain, Australia, New Zealand, India, and West Indies. Published works include: *Key to the Bible* (3 vols.), *The Path of Biblical Theology, Christ and Life, Spirit of the Living God, The New Guide to Reading and Studying the Bible, Mark* (Volume 4 of the *New Testament Message* series), and *Jesus and Paul: Signs of Contradiction.*

First published in 1988 by Michael Glazier, Inc., 1935 West Fourth Street, Wilmington, Delaware 19805. Distributed outside the U.S., Canada and Philippines by Dominican Publications, St. Saviour's, Upper Dorset St., Dublin.

Library of Congress Catalog Card Number: 87-82813
International Standard Book Number: 0-89453-649-4 (Michael Glazier)
0 907 271-85-5 (Dominican Publications)

Typography by Angela Meades.
Printed in the United States of America.

IN MEMORY OF
J. J.
MY NEPHEW

Being perfected in a short time,
he fulfilled long years (Wis 4:13).

CONTENTS

INTRODUCTION

THREE CHRISTMAS STORIES

The Christmas story is perhaps the best known, certainly the most popular, of our christian stories. This is particularly so in Roman Catholic tradition through familiarity with the Christmas crib. A childhood memory of a foremost Catholic theologian is eloquent. Edward Schillebeeckx is replying to the question: "When did your first hear about Jesus?"

> The first thing I remember about my childhood—what came to the surface at once, as soon as you asked that question—is the enormous crib that we had at home every Christmas. It stood in one corner of the drawing-room on a large table. It was a kind of cabin made of brown paper to imitate rocks. It wasn't life-size, but it was very big. There were a lot of figures, a whole caravansarai of camels, the three kings and, of course, the crib itself.[1]

---

[1] *God is New Each Moment* (New York: The Seabury Press, 1983, 2).

Many of us share that or a similar experience. In my childhood—rural Ireland—a family crib was not part of our tradition: the crib belonged in the church. Somehow, it was then even more evocative. We were familiar with the rather forbidding crucifix; we accepted, with awe, that Jesus was in the tabernacle, behind the flickering red flame; then, for a little while, he seemed so much closer: a wistful baby lying on straw. Though surrounded by an adoring Mary, Joseph and shepherds—not to mention the ox and donkey—he was the focus-point, refreshingly human. I do believe that I have been influenced, more than I realised, by the encouraging humanness of it all. It may, in some measure, account for my growing concern with the humanity of this son of man whom I believe, firmly, to be indeed Immanuel, God-with-us. The introduction, at Epiphany, of the "three kings" into that domestic scene did not spoil the effect. That baby had made an impact not to be impaired by those regal figures.

I am happy to acknowledge that the Christmas crib still pulls at my heartstrings. I am aware, of course, that it tells a Christmas story that never happened just like that. It is a third story built on two others—those of Matthew and Luke—touched by later embellishments. There are so many questions. Was Jesus born on 25 December? Was he born in Bethlehem because Joseph and Mary lived there (Matthew) or because they had journeyed from Nazareth (Luke)? Did a heavenly choir acclaim his birth (Luke)? Was he acknowledged by Judean shepherds (Luke) or Gentile "magi" (Matthew)? Did the family return peaceably to Nazareth shortly after the birth of Jesus (Luke) or did they have to spend a period of exile in Egypt (Matthew)?

So many questions—but not of great importance. Our

Christmas story is not historically precise—but neither are the stories of Matthew or Luke. My view, as a professional exegete, is that beyond the basic facts there is little that is strictly historical in the infancy gospels of Matthew and Luke; of course there is even less in *our* story which carries further embellishment. The stories of Matthew and Luke are quite independent of each other. Agreement between them is all the more impressive. The common story has Joseph, of Davidic descent, betrothed to Mary. Both evangelists agree on the virginal conception of Jesus and on the heavenly word that his name be Jesus, which means Savior. Jesus was born, after Mary and Joseph had come to live together, in Bethlehem; the child was raised at Nazareth. What this adds up to is that the heart-core of our cherished Christmas story is rock firm. But this is, of course, only if one finds oneself in a position to put the right question to each infancy gospel. At an early stage of my biblical studies I had the good fortune to happen on, or to hear (I have never been sure which) a statement that has proved immensely helpful: "When one of our western culture hears a story, the spontaneous reaction is: 'Is it true?' When a Semite hears a story his spontaneous question is: 'What does it mean?'" Just think of Jesus' parables and savor the wisdom of the observation. We want the infancy stories of Matthew and Luke to be wholly historical. What we have to face is the fact that neither is conventionally historical—nor was ever intended to be.

THE NATURE OF THE INFANCY GOSPELS

The infancy Gospels of Matthew and Luke have had a

notable influence on christian tradition and have put a profound mark on christian art. The high christian appreciation of them has not been misplaced. We had sensed that there was something special here—that these texts said a lot more than they appeared to say. In our day we have, happily, come to realise that both infancy narratives are, first and foremost, christological statements. It is along this line, and only here, that we can hope to grasp the true meaning of these remarkable texts.

Christology.

We are heirs of a sophisticated christology. We can too easily forget that our first brethren in the faith had to grapple with the awesome implications of their growing conviction that the risen Jesus belonged in the divine sphere, that he stood side by side with the only God. It could be no easy task to reconcile monotheism with such a perception of the risen Jesus. It would seem that, in the beginning, the resurrection was the chief moment associated with the divine proclamation of the identity of Jesus. Acts of the Apostles is formal: God raised up Jesus and *made* him Lord and Christ (2:32-36); God, at the resurrection, *exalted* him as Leader and Savior (5:30-31); Jesus is *begotten* as God's Son through the resurrection (13:32-33). And there is the important pre-Pauline creedal formula in Rom 1:3-4—". . . the gospel concerning his Son, who was descended from David according to the flesh and *designated* Son of God in power according to a Holy Spirit by resurrection from the dead." Through human origin Jesus is son of David, while through resurrection, Holy Spirit and power, Jesus is designated uniquely God's Son. Encounter with the risen Lord had opened the eyes of the disciples: this Jesus was Son of God.

This perception was the beginning of christology—the theological understanding of Jesus. As time passed awareness grew that what Jesus was seen to be after he resurrection he must have been before. What followed was a casting of the understanding and titles of the risen Christ back to Jesus of Nazareth in the gospel account of his earthly ministry. For Mark the baptism of Jesus is that moment of truth. "And when he came out of the water, immediately he saw the heavens opened and the Spirit descending upon him like a dove; and a voice from heaven, 'Thou art my beloved Son; with thee I am well pleased'" (Mk 1:10-11). By the device of a heavenly voice the evangelist is communicating to the christian reader God's revelation about who Jesus is. The Holy Spirit descends on him so that he can begin his ministry with power: an echo of Rom 1:3-4. Christological language, first related to the resurrection, is thus attached to the baptism of Jesus.

Matthew and Luke reach behind the baptism. Their earlier stage is found in their respective infancy gospels where understanding of Jesus as Messiah, Son of David, Savior, Lord and so on is pushed back to the infancy period. It represents a stage in the developing understanding of him who is the christian Lord: he is Lord not only in and through the resurrection, not only during his ministry, but also from the beginning of his earthly existence. The final step in New Testament christology was the Johannine one to pre-existence and incarnation: "In the beginning was the Word and the Word was with God...And the Word became flesh and dwelt among us" (Jn 1:1, 14). It might seem that, in comparison, the christology even of the infancy gospels is somehow inferior. Not so. *Logos* (Word) and "pre-existence" *sound* very impressive—but what do they mean? I would argue that the christology of Mark and the infancy-gospel christology of Matthew and Luke have no reason to defer to the christology of John. Their understanding of Jesus is not less sophisticated—it is different.

What is undeniable is that the infancy gospels are primarily concerned with christology. This is the insight which gives them enormous importance—and explains, perhaps, why, as I have observed, Christians have always been conscious of something special about them. At the same time one must recognise that Jesus is not the only character in these stories. By any standard the infancy gospels (Mt 1-2; Lk 1-2) are sophisticated literary texts. Of course they have, in the past, suffered from a view that they were pretty Christmas stories. Here, I plan to look at them as I would like to believe their authors had envisaged them. The result could be exciting.

As stories, our infancy gospels have plot and characters. The "star," of course, is, Jesus himself. But there is a host of other characters, many of them colorful. It will be instructive to look at them more closely, and to give flesh and blood to some who are in the text only as names. I have something further in mind: to see something of ourselves in the characters of the Christmas story. In short, I want to make two points. Firstly, a realisation of the fact that the infancy gospels are christological rather than historical enhances their importance. Secondly, that we have much to learn from the lively characters of these brilliant stories.

Drama.

I have mentioned plot and character. I think it helpful to view the infancy gospels as drama—no one will deny their dramatic dimension. At any rate, I give here a list of the dramatis personae.

THE INFANCY GOSPELS
Dramatic Personae.

MATTHEW

The Star	The Child Jesus
Leading Actors	Joseph—Mary
	The Magi
	Herod
Supporting Actors	Chief Priests and Scribes
Hidden Actors	Abraham
	Jacob
	Tamar, Rahab, Ruth, Bathsheba.
	Ahaz
	Manasseh
Deus Ex Machina	The Angel*

LUKE

The Stars	The Children: Jesus and John
Leading Actors	The Parents: Mary [Joseph],
	Zechariah and Elizabeth

*This angel and the angels of Luke are conventional: a stereotyped biblical way of communicating heavenly messages. The word *angelos* means "messenger."

Supporting Actors	The Shepherds
	Simeon
	Anna
Hidden Actor	Caesar Augustus
Dei Ex Machina	Gabriel
	An Angel of the Lord
	The Heavenly Host

An intriguing feature is that the "stars" are wholly passive and silent throughout! The passage Lk 2:41-51, where Jesus does act and speak, is not really an exception. This "finding in the Temple" episode is an evident appendix to an *infancy* narrative.

THE ANCESTRY OF JESUS

Matthew's Genealogy

"THE BOOK OF THE GENEALOGY OF JESUS CHRIST"

The Old Testament, in particular Genesis and First Chronicles, makes skillful and varied use of genealogies. In his turn Matthew finds his genealogy to be an effective way of establishing the identity of Jesus. Jesus is a son of Israel; further he is the fulfillment of a history guided by God. Matthew combines both themes by presenting Jesus as the Messianic king, tracing his ancestry back through David's line. In the main, he turned to the Scriptures, finding in 1 Chr 2:1-5 and Ruth 4:18-22 his sources for 1:2-6a and in 1, 2 Kings the list of kings given in 1:6b-11. First Chr 19-14 and a popular genealogy of the Davidic Messiah provided the names in 1:12-16—to which Matthew added Joseph, Mary and Jesus.

Matthew's pattern of three sets of 14 generations is patently artificial; to get his "fourteen generations from David to the Exile" he passed over in silence some of the kings of Judah. He appears to have been influenced by current apocalyptic thought which cast world history in periods of sevens, in other words, "weeks" of years. For Israel's history Matthew counts "two 'weeks' of generations (2 x 7 = 14 generations), from Israel's beginnings in Abraham to its high point in *King* David, two more weeks from its high point to its low point in the disaster of the Babylonian exile, and two further weeks during its ascent to its goal, Jesus the Messiah. Jesus Christ thus begins the seventh period, the period of perfection and fulfillment (cf. Daniel's seventy weeks of years in Dan 9). Hence Matthew uses an apocalyptic convention to proclaim that God has secretly ordered the economy of salvation so that all of Israel's history moves smoothly towards the Messiah."[1]

One must be aware that this Jesus is not only son of David—he is also "the son of Abraham." As such he is fulfillment of the promise that through Abraham "all the nations" of the earth would be blessed (Gen 12:3; 22:18). Significantly, the gospel closes with the commission to "make disciples of all nations" (Mt 28:19). With his designation of Jesus as "the son of David, the son of Abraham," Matthew is declaring the Messiah to be the Savior (v 21) of Jew and Gentile.

When one looks at Matthew's list, one finds a mixed bag. To an extent we are faced with names only. But we can put faces on a goodly number of the names—and not all are prepossessing. Jesus' ancestry is not a saintly line; it is, in generous measure, disreputable. True, it begins on a high note, with Abraham the man of faith—who is followed by a weak Isaac and a rascally Jacob. It is comforting to stress this aspect of the genealogy. One might say that Matthew is, in his way,

[1]John P. Meier, *Matthew* (Wilmington, DE: M. Glazier, 1980), 3-4.

making the same point as the author of Hebrews: the sinless Jesus is "like his brethren in every respect" (Heb 2:17). He had no control over his ancestry. There is, too, the comforting assurance that God "can write straight on crooked lines," that inadequate humans cannot thwart his purpose; they may indeed serve his purpose.

Abraham to David

ABRAHAM, MAN OF FAITH

In Genesis the story of Abraham (12:1—25:18) and the story of Jacob form two contrasting blocks. Isaac is found in both but as a pale figure: son of Abraham and father of Jacob, and little more than that. Behind the two story cycles stand vague memories of Israel's semi-nomadic ancestors: of an "Abraham" tribe and a "Jacob" tribe. In the Genesis saga the "tribes" yield to the neat genealogy of Abraham, Isaac, Jacob and the Twelve. The origin of Israel, like that of all peoples, was complex. Here is later Israel's powerful statement of its national identity. In the stories as we have them—and Matthew would have taken them at face value—Abraham and Jacob are painted in vivid colors. Reading in his manner, we may see what we can make of them.

From the start, Abraham is the man of faith. In Gen 12:1 he is called upon to break with all natural ties, starting with the most general: country, clan and family. Yahweh is fully aware of the difficulty of what he asks: Abraham must leave everything. And he must go "to the land that I will show you";

the demand on the faith of Abraham is radical. The author of Hebrews has a perceptive comment: "By faith Abraham obeyed when he was called to go to a place which he was to receive as an inheritance; and he went out, not knowing where he was to go" (Heb 11:8). Later, despite the advanced age of Abraham and Sarah and her barrenness, Abraham puts his faith in Yahweh, confident that he will be ancestor of numberless descendants (Gen 15:5-6). And then there is the "sacrifice" of Abraham—his readiness to sacrifice the child of promise, Isaac (22:1-19). After all this it is encouraging to discover that Abraham has his weak side. He is prepared to jeopardize Sarai to save his own skin (12:10-20). And when he first heard the promise of the birth of Isaac he reacted with amused incredulity (17:15-16). Still, the verdict of Paul stands: Abraham is man of faith (Gal 3:6-9; Rom 4:1-3).

JACOB, MAN OF GUILE

Jacob is a very different character. The Jacob-stories are laced with humor—sometimes black humor. From the start the astuteness of Jacob is signalled: born second of a pair of twins, he came from the womb with a firm grip on Esau's heel (Gen 25:26). We are not surprised to learn that he will trick poor Esau out of his birthright—his right of primogeniture, of firstborn (25:29-34). Jacob has a capable ally in his mother Rebekah; he is her favorite. A blind Isaac sensed the approach of death and craved one good meal before the end. He asked Esau (his favorite) to hunt down game and cook it for him. Rebekah had taken care to overhear the request and determined to turn it to her darling's advantage. The subterfuge of covering the smooth hands and neck of Jacob with goat-skins so that he might pass for the hairy Esau certainly calls for a "suspension of disbelief"! But the trick worked and Jacob received the blessing of the firstborn. Esau and Isaac had been outwitted (27:1-40). It might seem to us that Isaac, when he had realised the deception, could simply have, as it were, altered his will. The point of the story is that a blessing, once bestowed, could not be withdrawn. Rebekah had played on that, and had won. So it was that Jacob became ancestor of the Twelve Tribes of Israel.

The story continues in a similar vein. Jacob felt it prudent to get out of range of an understandably peeved Esau and went off to his uncle Laban in Haran. Trickery ran in the family and we have a battle of wits between uncle and nephew (29:1-32:2), with Jacob winning out. Yet again he was able to out-maneuver his brother Esau (32:3–33:17). Altogether, not a savoury character. Still, he has his good points. There is his prayer (32:9-12) as he fearfully prepares to meet his brother. He protests: "O Lord . . . I am not worthy of the least of all the steadfast love and all the faithfulness which you have shown to your servant" (v 10). Earlier, on his way to Haran, he had his dream at Bethel—the dream of Jacob's ladder: "He dreamed that there was a ladder set up on the earth, and the top of it reached to heaven; and behold, the angels of God were ascending and descending on it!" (28:12). It is a meeting place of God and humankind. Then there is the strange episode of Jacob's wrestling-bout with God (32:24-32) when he is told: "you have striven with God and with men, and have prevailed" (v 28). A Jacob who had adeptly dealt with men (Esau, Isaac, Laban) has successfully contended with God. "He has learnt that a genuine relationship with God does not reside in mere passivity, rejoicing in election and waiting on providence (the prayer in 32:1-13); it entails as well personal effort, a striving, wrestling with the divine will and purposes."[2] Jacob had matured, had grown in wisdom.

What matters most is that from the first, though he seemed unpromising material, he was vehicle of the divine promise. Though he had stolen his father's blessing, it was a blessing, and was repeated as Isaac sent him off to Laban (28:3-5). In his Bethel dream he heard the assurance: "the land on which you lie I will give to you and your descendants; and your descendants shall be like the dust of the earth, and you shall spread abroad to the west and to east and to the north and to the south; and by you and your descendants shall all the families of the earth bless themselves" (28:13-14). Later, again at Bethel, the promise was repeated (35:9-13), finally, before his departure for Egypt to find a home with Joseph he was comforted at Beersheba:

> I am God, the God of your father; do not be afraid to go down to Egypt; for I will there make of you a great nation. I will go down with you to Egypt, and I will also bring you up again (46:3-4).

Jacob's native cunning would have availed him nothing if his God had not been with him.

THE FOUR WOMEN

A fascinating feature of Matthew's genealogy is the prominence of women in his list. One would have expected Mary,

---

[2]Bruce Vawter, *On Genesis. A New Reading* (London: G. Chapman, 1977), 351.

of course, but not the others: Tamar, Rahab, Ruth, Bathsheba. Their presence is due to the fact that they are "holy irregularities": there is something not quite regular in the relationship of each with her spouse. Tamar (Gen 38) is an obvious example. She had been married to Er, son of Judah, who died without issue. According to levirate law (Dt 25:5-6) it was the duty of the next son, Onan, to marry the widow; the first son of that union would be regarded as son of the deceased, so guaranteeing the only immortality he might have.[3] Onan was not happy with the arrangement and challenged it—with fatal results. Judah had lost two of his three sons; he was not going to risk the third. It became clear to Tamar that Judah had no intention of following through on his levirate obligation so she determined to take the law into her own hands. She tricked her father-in-law into becoming father of the twins Perez and Zerah. And Judah had to acknowledge: "She is more righteous than I" (38:26).

As for the other women: Rahab was a prostitute (Jos 2:1-21) and Bathsheba was an adulteress (2 Sam 11:2-5)—hence at least some "scandal" attached to them. In the case of Ruth, the passage Ruth 3:6-14 might give rise to some suspicion as to the relationship between Ruth and Boaz. Each in her own manner then, these women were foils to Mary and her "holy irregularity"—virginal conception. But there is more to it. These women played an important role in God's plan—observe the initiative of Rahab and Ruth; all four of them continued the lineage of the Messiah. In that line of the Messiah Matthew had clearly seen the hand of God.

[3]One should note that not until the second century B.C. was there, in Israel, any real notion of an afterlife; life ended in the gloom of Sheol—in effect, the grave.

David to the Exile

DAVID—THE FLAWED SAINT

We may leave aside the stories about the young David (1 Sam 16:1—19:7) and his outlaw career (1 Sam 19:8—2 Sam 1). His days of flight and forced brigandage over, we read in 2 Sam 2-8 of how David came to be king, first of Judah and then of the united kingdom of Judah and Israel. He had won for himself the Canaanite stronghold of Jerusalem and made it his capital—the City of David (2 Sam 5). By installing the ark of Yahweh there he turned it into the religious center of his domain. Then, adverting to the incongruity that he had a palace while the ark of Yahweh was still housed in a tent, he planned to build a temple, but was told by the prophet Nathan that the temple was not to be his achievement. The Lord had pre-empted his plan. David had hoped to build a house (temple) for Yahweh; instead, it is Yahweh who would build a house (dynasty) for David (7:4-17). "And your house and your kingdom shall be made sure for ever before me; your throne shall be established for ever" (7:16). In a long and moving prayer (7:18-29) David thanks the Lord for his favor.

Before long we are sharply reminded that David has his weak side. He cast his eye on Bathsheba, wife of one of his officers, and committed adultery with her. It is clear that the affair was an open secret; the husband Uriah was aware that he had been cuckolded (11:1-13). David's next move was wholly unworthy of one who before, and again, displayed greatness—he engineered the death of Uriah (11:12-25). It was cold-blooded murder. The redeeming feature is that, when chal-

lenged by a prophet, David acknowledged his double sin
(12:1-15). The prophet obviously expected the confession and
repentance of his king—not even the king might flout the law
of Yahweh. And it is to David's credit that he saw it so. He
made no excuses. The sequel shows him free once more of his
disastrous aberration and measuring up to his true stature.

We observe this in the marvelously vivid narrative of
12:15-23—David's prayer for his stricken child, the child of
his adultery with Bathsheba. The gifted author of the Court
History (the narrative 2 Sam 9-20 + 1 Kg 1-2) is at his best.
David had prayed and fasted while the child still lived. On
learning of his death he, to the amazement of his servants,
washed, changed his clothes, and ate for the first time in a
week. He explained his surprising conduct:

> While the child was still alive, I fasted and wept, for I said,
> "Who knows whether the Lord will be gracious to me, that the
> child may live?" But now he is dead; why should I fast? Can I
> bring him back again? I shall go to him, but he will not return to
> me (12:15-23).

It is David's finest hour.

David had confessed and repented, but he had sown his
dragon's teeth; he must reap the harvest of bitter family strife.
For all his greatness he was flesh and blood and knew his times
of frailty and of failure. We have seen something of that
weakness. We learn that the gifted statesman who could
achieve and maintain the unity of two kingdoms (Judah and
Israel) was a disaster as a family man. He barely escaped not
only replacement but death as well at the hands of his favorite,
the handsome and arrogant Absalom (13:1—19:8). Moving
indeed is the king's anguish at the death of this son who had
sought his life:

> And the king was deeply moved, and went up to the chamber
> over the gate, and wept; and as he went, he said, "O my son
> Absalom, my son, my son Absalom! Would I had died instead of
> you, O Absalom, my son, my son!" (18:33).

The story of David ends on a sad note (1 Kgs 1). We see him, "old and advanced in years." He is out of touch, and his plans for the succession were almost circumvented by another ambitious son, Adonijah. The redoubtable Bathsheba, ably supported by the prophet Nathan, thwarted the attempted coup and brought her son Solomon (David's nominee) to the throne. It is, or might be, disturbing to hear David's last commission to the new king. He wants him to deal with Joab, his veteran friend and army commander, a man who had been guilty of two political assassinations. And he instructs him to kill, too, the Shimei who had cursed David as he fled from Absalom, cf. 2 Sam 16:5-12 (1 Kgs 2:5-9). David was a man of his time. Murder had to be avenged, and Joab was guilty. Curse was efficacious unless turned against its originator. We must measure David by the standards of his day.

We take our leave of David the scarred warrior and marred follower of Yahweh. The verdict of Hamlet on his father is apposite: "he was a man, take him for all in all . . . ." At any rate, the lusty and vulnerable David of 2 Samuel is so much more congenial than the "saint" of 1 Chronicles 11-29—that a typical piece of hagiography. Surely we would find more encouragement in the flawed hero of 2 Samuel than in the white-power knight of Chronicles.

The House of David

The author of the Books of Kings passes judgment on the kings of Judah. Only eight of them receive praise, six of them, however, with qualification. Hezekiah and Josiah alone merit unreserved approval. Both were reformers; and Josiah had set about centralizing the cult in Jerusalem. "One God, one sanctuary" is a fundamental article of Deuteronomy, and judgment on the kings is inspired by that viewpoint. It is a concrete way of demanding individual loyalty to a "jealous" God and unwavering fidelity to his commands. In keeping with our interest here, stressing the "disreputable" lineage of the Messiah, we shall look to two less favored kings.

AHAZ

Ahaz (740-736 B.C.) was king of Judah in a time of crisis when the throne of David was in jeopardy. The kings of Israel and Damascus had formed a league against the Assyrian superpower; Ahaz refused to be drawn into the league. The allies declared war, meaning to overthrow Ahaz and place on the throne of Judah a creature of their own, a certain "son of Tabeel." Jerusalem was besieged (Is 7:1-6). Isaiah counseled his king to put his trust in Yahweh (7:7-9). The king's refusal to seek a sign of assurance (vv 10-12) came, not from piety (though he feigned piety), but because he had already made up his mind to reject the prophet's advice. Threatened as he was, he had determined to invite the intervention of the Assyrians; he had no confidence in the help of Yahweh. One does not so easily dispose of God: Ahaz will have his sign whether he wills or not. Isaiah had taken his stand on God's covenant with David (2 Sam 7). Each successive king of David's line personified the covenant relationship; each was a living reminder and guarantee of the covenant. Ahaz' queen is, at this moment of crisis, pregnant with the one who will continue the threatened line: "The young woman is with child and will bear a son, and will call his name Immanuel" (Is 7:14). But Ahaz had shown himself to be at best an agnostic, at worst an unbeliever. Though heir to David's throne he did not share the faith of David.

MANASSEH

The long reign of Manasseh (687-642 B.C.) was disastrous for the religion of Yahweh. The reforms of his father Hezekiah had not been popular; now there was a strong reaction. Besides, under Ashurbanipal, Assyria was at the height of its power and its influence was felt in the cultic and religious field; as a faithful vassal, Manasseh sought to please his masters. Even so, his loyalty seemed suspect and he was sent in chains to Babylon. He was released after a few years. On his return he tried to do something about restoring the religion of Yahweh.

The Chronicler alone tells of Manasseh's conversion and makes reference to his prayer of repentance (2 Chr 33:1-20). A fruit of this reference is the apocryphal Prayer of Manasseh. It is a worthy example of post-exilic piety, a prayer of repentance more moving than the *Miserere*. It rings with serene confidence in a merciful God:

> You are the Lord Most High, of great compassion, long-suffering and very merciful, and repent over the evils of men. You, O Lord, according to your great goodness have promised repentance and forgiveness to those who have sinned against you; and in the multitude of your mercies you have appointed repentance for sinners, that they may be saved . . . you have appointed repentance for me who am a sinner . . . And now I bend the knee of my heart beseeching you for your kindness . . . for you, O Lord, are the God of those who repent.

The message seems to be that if even *Manasseh* (cf. 2 Kgs 21:1-18; 2 Chr 33:1-9) could, having turned back to the Lord, feel confident of salvation, there is hope for any and every sinner! Perhaps, after all, that psalm may reflect the truth of the situation, for Manasseh was a trapped man. King of tiny and helpless Judah, he was vassal of the ruthless Assyrian empire—and Assyria demanded total subservience. The author of Kings is unforgiving; it may be that the Chronicler has not only been kinder but has also been more fair.

After the Exile

Jeremiah and Ezekiel have documented the lamentable religious situation during the last years of Judah. The nation seemed hell-bent on destruction. The tragic years are hidden under Matthew's phrase, "Jechoniah [Jehoiachin] and his brothers . . ." The list continues, "after the deportation to Babylon." There could be another form of infidelity. Israel might be untrue to its vocaton not only through gross sinfulness but by insularity, by failure to fulfull its mission.

The history of life in Judah after the return was to show

that, sadly, the glowing vision of Second Isaiah (Is 40-55) was lost to sight. The community had found its way but, more and more, that way became *its* way. No longer was there gross infidelity. Indeed, fidelity became an obsession. Faithfulness lay in meticulous observance of commandments, statutes and ritual. It followed that God could no longer be, truly, a universal God. He could only be the God of those who served him according to the minutiae of Torah.

Conclusion

Matthew's genealogy has told the reader that Jesus is "son of David" and "son of Abraham." Matthew leaves the "son of Abraham" motif and its Gentile connotation until the story of the magi (Mt 2:1-12) and concentrates first on son of David. What emerges is that Jesus is of the Messianic line. What we have been at pains to show is that he is of *this* line. Here is documentation to back up the assertion in Hebrews that he is like us in all things. Jesus of Nazareth is of the human family of David; Jesus the Savior is of the human race. There is our comfort and our hope.

My lingering over sinners and flawed saints in the ancestral line of the Messiah is not morbid. I have prepared for the final chapter where I will suggest that we may recognize ourselves among such people. We are called to be holy, but few of us are holy. No cause for despondency, however. As there was hope for a Manasseh there is hope for any of us. All because Jesus, born of a sinful line, "will save his people from their sins."

2

THE PEOPLE OF
THE INFANCY GOSPELS

Having looked behind the names in Matthew's genealogy, we come to the drama proper—rather to the two dramas: of Matthew and of Luke. Here we find more than names; here characters are sketched, some vividly, others faintly. We hope to help the reader of the stories to discern the characters more clearly and appreciate their significance.

JOSEPH

In building his infancy narrative Matthew has made use of two main blocks of material: a cycle of angelic dream appearances and the magi story. The material has been thoroughly edited by the evangelist, but the two blocks are still recognisably distinct.*

---

*For the structure and other aspects of the Infancy Gospels I am much indebted to Raymond E. Brown [*The Birth of the Messiah*] (New York: Doubleday, 1977)]

The pattern of Angelic Dream Appearances (A. 1:20; 1:21. B. 2:13-15a. C. 2:19-21, 22-23).

(A) 1:20   As he was considering this, behold . . .

(B) 2:13   When they had gone away, behold . . .

(C) 2:19   When Herod died, behold . . .

(1)   An angel of the Lord appeared to Joseph in a dream (1:20; 2:13; 2:19).

(2)   The angel gave a *command*: A. 1:20; 1:21; B. 2:13; C. 2:20)

(3)   The angel offered a *reason* for the command: A. 1:20; 1:21; B. 2:13; C. 2:20.

(4)   Joseph rose and *fulfilled* the command: A. 1:24-25; B. 2:14-15a; C. 2:21.

Joseph wears the cloak of the famous patriarch Joseph (Gen 37-50), especially in his being a man of dreams and in his going down to Egypt.

PERPLEXED AND JUST (Mt 1:18-25)

Joseph and Mary were betrothed. In Jewish society, betrothal was something far more serious than our marriage engagement. Betrothal was really a marriage contract, except that the partners had not begun to live together. Joseph discovered that his betrothed was pregnant. "Of the Holy Spirit" is Matthew's nod to the reader; Joseph was not aware of that factor and was in a quandary. He was a "just" and "upright" man, a Jew who took Torah seriously. He assumed that Mary had been unfaithful. The death penalty for adultery (Dt 22:20-21) was not then, if it ever had been, in force; divorce was the answer. This was the course Joseph decided on—except that he wanted to divorce her "quietly." It is not clear how he could have hoped to achieve this. And divorce would not have helped Mary at all. She would have been left on her own to bear her baby—in a thoroughly disapproving society. The "just" man, Joseph, was a confused man. He desperately wanted to do the decent thing, but his "solution" was no solution at all.

Happily for him—and for Mary—God took a hand. In a dream, all was made clear. Mary was not an unfaithful bride but a wholly privileged instrument of God. Her child, of divine parenthood, would be Savior; the one who "will save his people from their sins." And here Matthew throws in his formula-citation.[1] He looked to Is 7:14 (in the Greek) and found there a word of promise: "the virgin would bear a son." That son will be Emmanuel, God-with-us. Cleverly, Matthew has anticipated the close of his gospel: "Lo, I am with you always" (Mt 28:20). In that unique child of Mary, a first-century Palestinian Jew, we meet our God. Paul has put it in his inimitable fashion: "God was in Christ, reconciling the world to himself" (2 Cor 5:19).

DISPLACED PERSONS (Mt 2:13-15)

Herod had designs on Mary's child. Joseph was bidden to take "the child and his mother" to the safety of Egypt. The formula citation from Hos 11:1, "Out of Egypt have I called my son," makes clear Matthew's intention. Jesus was re-enacting the sojourn of his people in Egypt. Here, too, though in a different manner, the journey was managed by a Joseph

[1]See p. 74.

(Gen 45:16–47:12). The question must be raised: was there a flight into Egypt? One asks the question because there is no place for it in Luke's infancy story. Luke declares that after the baby's presentation in the Temple, forty days after his birth, they (Joseph, Mary and the child) "returned into Galilee, to their own city, Nazareth" (Lk 2:39). It is likely that Matthew, in true midrash tradition,[2] had elaborated on the Hosean text. What matters is that the "holy family" are cast as displaced persons. What matters is the theological rather than the historical dimension. The vulnerability of Emmanuel—God-with-us—is underlined. And that means the vulnerability of God. God is firmly on the side of the oppressed, not of the oppressor. He is a God who displays a preferential option for the poor.

The return, too, was sad (Mt 2:19-23). In Matthew, Bethlehem was the home of Joseph and Mary. Displaced persons, yearning to go home, they think it safe to return to Palestine. Sadly, they cannot go back to their home town—they must go on to Nazareth. One looks at a map of Palestine and thinks: what a big deal! The fact is, Judea and Galilee, though geographically close, were different in many respects. Besides, there can be a world of difference between two contiguous districts. Whether we are urbanites or country-dwellers we are surely aware of that. Joseph had come back to his own land, and found himself a stranger there.

[2]Midrash—from the verb darash, to "search out"—was a familiar Jewish use of Scripture. It could vary from an explanation of a text to a story built on a text.

THE OPPOSITION

Herod (Mt 2:1-8, 13-18)

Herod the Great was, by grace of Rome, king of Palestine 37-4 B.C. Although he never gained the affection, or even respect, of his Jewish subjects (who regarded him as a "half-Jew" in view of his Idumean origin), he was an able and energetic ruler, at least in Roman eyes. In the domestic sphere, his reign was very troubled. Of a suspicious nature (in 29 B.C. he had his favorite wife, Mariamne, executed for alleged adultery), he was jealous of his power and reacted violently against any suspect attempt on it. In 28 B.C. his mother-in-law was put to death on the charge of plotting against him. In 7 B.C. Alexander and Aristobulus, his sons by Mariamne, were strangled. A few days before his death, the king had his son Antipater executed.

This Herod is recognisable in the Herod of Matthew. But the evangelist, in his sketch of Herod, has also been influenced by the Exodus story of Moses and the Pharaoh; the parallel is obvious enough. The Pharaoh had sought Moses' life; the latter had fled for safety. The Pharaoh had commanded that all male Hebrew infants be cast into the Nile. After the death of Pharaoh, Moses was bidden to return from exile "for all those who were seeking your life are dead" (Ex 4:19). Herod sought the life of the infant Messiah, who was carried off to safety. After the death of Herod, Joseph was told to return to the land of Egypt, "for those who sought the child's life are dead" (Mt 2:20). The basic story-line 2:13-15 concerns the rescue of the child savior from the machinations of the wicked king by flight into Egypt. Jewish tradition, as we find it, for instance, in Flavius Josephus, had it that the Pharaoh of the Exodus had been forewarned, by one of his "sacred scribes." of the birth of a Hebrew who would constitute a threat to the Egyptian kingdom. In another version, the warning came in a dream interpreted by his "magi." Pharaoh and the whole of Egypt were filled with dread (cf. Mt 2:3). Pharaoh's plan to dispose of the threat was frustrated by a warning communicated in a dream to Moses' father. The Moses-legend surely has colored the Matthean narrative.

Matthew's Herod is not an attractive character, he is a conniving man, and a man who can fly into a murderous rage. His feigned piety reminds one of Ahaz; he would worship this blessed child! When his strategem failed, he ordered the massacre of innocent infants. Yet, despite his power over life and death, he is weak, insecure. He is not unlike the Pilate portrayed by John (Jn 18:28–19:16).

Chief Priests and Scribes (Mt 2:4-6)

Matthew has introduced "all the chief priests and scribes of the people" as advisers of the sinister Herod. It might appear that they do no more than answer a theological question. Matthew certainly implies something else. In the first place, they, too, had been "troubled" by the magis' word of birth of the Messiah. They could not have been deceived by Herod's feigned peity. Knowing that he was paranoid on the subject of any threat to his throne, they should have realised that he would not look kindly upon an infant "king of the Jews." By disclosing to him the birthplace of the Messiah they became, effectively, collaborators in his evil intent. In fact it is they, not Herod, who will bring about the death of the "king of the Jews." It is "the chief priests and elders of the people" who will plot to arrest and kill Jesus (26:3-5, 47; 27:1-2, 12, 20); "the scribes" are mentioned in 26:57 and 27:41. They are those who have their own understanding of religion; they are those who jealously guard their status and privilege. Cf. Jn 11:48. Such as they cannot be open to the word of this birth, as they will not be open to the message of Jesus. Such as they will want to get rid of him. He was a threat to Herod and to them: to the throne of one, to the religious empire of the others.

THE MAGI (Mt 2:1-12)

One could read and understand the second chapter of Matthew without reference to the first, and the same is true of Luke's second chapter in relation to his first. Interestingly, too, Bethlehem is mentioned for the first time in these second chapters and both close with a move to Nazareth. In his narrative, Matthew has cast back into the infancy the reactions that, historically, greeted the proclamation of the risen Lord: some believed and paid homage; others rejected both the message and the preachers. In other words, christological revelation was followed by proclamation and by the twofold reaction of acceptance-homage and rejection-persecution. But this had been prepared for in the ministry of Jesus. The same pattern is presented in the infancy narrative. The negative reaction (of Herod and his advisers, the chief priests and scribes) turns the infancy narrative into a veritable gospel—for the gospel must have suffering and rejection as well as success.

As it stands, 2:1-12 is a self-contained story, with no mention of Joseph. There is little point in looking for the homeland of the magi, whom Matthew seemingly would regard as wise and learned Gentiles. Nor is there any point in looking to a comet, a supernova, or a planetary conjection to account for "his star" (1:20). A star which rises, goes before, and comes to rest over a place is no natural phenomenon. More to the point is the fact that, for Matthew, the magi represent the Gentiles, fittingly alerted not by an angel (as Luke's Jewish shepherds) but by a star. Their coming anticipates the promise of Jesus: "many will come from east and west and sit at table with Abraham, Isaac and Jacob in the kingdom of heaven" (8:11). The liturgical tradition of Epiphany has caught Matthew's intention.

The Balaam narrative of Numbers 22-24, embroidered with Jewish tradition, would, skillfully used by Matthew, appear to have been the inspiration of the magi story. Balaam, a seer, was summoned by Balak "from he east" to curse Israel. Significantly, the Alexandrian Jewish philosopher Philo calls him a magos. Herod tried to use the magi for his own ends as Balak had tried to get a magos to destroy his enemy, only to have him bless the enemy. Herod tried to manipulate the magi: they ended up worshiping the "enemy" he had sought to destroy. In his oracle, Balaam had declared:

> a star will come forth from Jacob, and a scepter will rise from Israel (Hebrew).

> a star will rise from Jacob, and a man will stand forth from Israel (Greek).

The oracle refers to David. Here, credibly, one looks for Matthew's star."

Matthew has the magi joyfully follow the guiding star to the house where they found child and mother—the house being the Bethlehem home of Joseph and Mary. Fittingly, they had brought gifts for the king: gifts of gold (Ps 72:10-15), frankincense (Is 60-6) and myrrh (like frankincense, an aromatic gum). The three gifts were, later, to suggest *three* magi (Matthew does not specify); and the gifts themselves were given symbolic meanings.

The Old Testament, and popular tradition based on it, form the basis of Matthew's magi story; its purpose is firmly christological. Our concern, though, is with the characters of the story: in this respect, the magi. They are Gentiles, illustrating the universal breadth of the good news brought by the "king of the Jews." They are people of good will, open to God, ready to hear and follow the call of God. They are people willing to follow a star, wherever it might lead. Open and starry-eyed, they are naive, guileless, easily taken-in by self-serving priests and murderous king. They are romantic and lovable figures.

ZECHARIAH (Lk 1:5-23)

Luke composed his infancy narrative in two stages. The first stage established a parallelism between the Baptist and Jesus.

I.   Two Annunciations of Conception

1. John the Baptist's annunciation (1:5-23) plus Elizabeth's pregnancy and praise of God.

2. Jesus' annunciation (1:26-38) plus Elizabeth's praise of Mary's pregnancy (1:39-45, 56).

II. Two Narratives of Birth-Circumcision-Naming and Future Greatness

> 1. Narrative about John the Baptist (1:57-66) plus a growth statement transitional to his ministry (1:80).
>
> 2. Narrative about Jesus (2:1-27, 34-39) plus a growth statement transitional to his ministry (2:40).

At the second stage Luke inserted the canticles (1:46-55 1:68-79; 2:29-32) and added the episode of the finding in the temple (2:41-52)—valuable material which, however, unbalanced the neat pattern of diptychs.

Zechariah was a Temple priest who belonged to the division of Abijah, the eighth of twenty-four divisions of priests (1 Chr 24:10) who carried out, in turn, the daily service of the temple. Zechariah and his wife were saintly Israelites who faithfully observed the commandments of God. Like Abraham and Sarah, he and his wife were elderly, and, humanly speaking, must remain childless. Hence the child to be born was in a special way a gift of God, a child of grace like Isaac, Samson and Samuel. Each division of priests served for a week at a time. Because of the great number of priests, the chief offices were assigned by lot. To Zechariah had fallen the highest priestly duty of burning fresh incense on the altar which stood before Holy of Holies. It was an auspicious moment for a divine message, and the messenger of the Lord, Gabriel, suddenly appeared in the place of honor at the right hand side of the altar. Zechariah's spontaneous reaction to the heavenly apparition was fear—the standard reaction in the presence of the heavenly. The angel reassured him; God had heard his prayer. The remainder of the verse makes it clear that the object of the prayer was, indeed, the birth of a son; though, in view of v 18, this had not been a recent prayer of the old priest.

Zechariah's request for a sign betrayed a certain skepticism (v 20). Gabriel is one of the seven "angels of the face" of Jewish tradition, who stand in the presence of God; he was sent by God to bring this "good news." The sign that Zechariah received was also a rebuke; he will be dumb (and deaf, v 62). The ceremony of offering incense was simple and brief and the people who awaited the priestly blessing wondered at the delay. When the priest emerged they recognised in his dumbness the effect of a vision, while he conveyed as much to them by signs. Zechariah was not one of the priests who lived in Jerusalem; his home was in a town in the hill country of Judea (1:39). Soon after, in line with the heavenly message, his wife Elizabeth conceived.

The birth of John (1:57-58) marked the fulfillment of the angel's message to Zechariah. Circumcision was prescribed for the eighth day after birth. It had become customary to name the child on that day and to celebrate the occasion by a party to which relatives and neighbors were invited. Zechariah confirmed that the child should be named John. Thereupon, he found himself able to speak again and again and his first words were a hymn of praise, the *Benedictus*.

Zechariah was a righteous man. He was human enough, however, to be taken aback by the startling word that, in old age, he will father a son—to be born of his elderly and barren wife! His skepticism must have sounded in his words. The ways of God can seem very strange, incredible indeed, even to a saintly man.

ELIZABETH (Lk 1:24-25–39-66)

Elizabeth is, like her husband, characterized as righteous and blameless. Her barrenness was not blameworthy in God's sight; but Elizabeth herself, a woman of her time and culture, had viewed it as her "disgrace" or "reproach" (1:25). At any rate she came to rejoice in what the Lord had wrought for her. She "hid herself" for five months, that her pregnancy unknown to any but herself and her husband—should be a striking sign for Mary (1:36) who would visit her in the sixth month of that pregnancy (1:26).

And Mary did duly visit her relative (1:39-44). The "city of Judah," in view of the determination "hill country," must be in the neighborhood of Jerusalem; a tradition, going back to the sixth century, points to the delightfully situated village of Ain Karim, five miles west of the city. At Mary's greeting Elizbeth felt the infant move in her womb (cf. Gen 25:22): he had leaped for joy at the presence of the mother of the Messiah (v 44). The Baptist in the womb is already a "prophet of the Most High"; it is through his prophetic action that Elizabeth knows Mary to be "the mother of my Lord" (1:43). As mother of the Messiah, Mary is "blessed among women," a Hebraism meaning the most blessed of women. Luke has based Elizabeth's blessing of Mary on the words of the woman in the crowd who had blessed the mother of Jesus and on Jesus' response: "Blessed is the womb that bore you . . . blessed are those who hear the word of God and keep it" (Lk 11:27-28). The blessing concerns Mary's role in God's saving plan. And so Elizabeth went on to praise Mary's unhesitating acquiescence in God's purpose—her great faith.

She was to have Mary's companionship and help for three

months. It is not at once clear that Mary left for home before the birth of the Baptist. Typically, the evangelist is rounding off one theme before passing to another. The Visitation episode did close with the departure of Mary, so he mentions it at the end; the birth of John is a distinct episode. John's birth, we have noted, marks the fulfillment of the angel's message to Zechariah (1:57-58). The completion of Elizabeth's term of pregnancy suggests, too, the fulfillment of messianic times. And the rejoicing of neighbors and kinsfolk is already an accomplishment of the promise of v 14.

Elizabeth, a pious and model Jewess, was privileged to be mother of the Baptist, the child of promise, the one who is to go before the Lord (v 17). It was her privilege, too, to welcome into her home the mother of the Messiah. Her insight singled out the faith of Mary: "blessed is she who believed." She, a woman, was the first in Luke's narrative (other than Mary) to know that the Messiah had come among his people.

THE SHEPHERDS (Lk 2:8-20)

In Lk 7:22 we learn that one of the signs given to the Baptist whereby he might know that Jesus was indeed the Messiah was that "the poor have good news preached to them." It is the climactic sign and so it is fitting that the first announcement of Jesus' birth was made to simple shepherds. These, the poor and humble, despised by the orthodox as non-observers of the Torah, are granted and accept the revelation which the leaders of Israel will reject.

Bethelehem lies at the edge of the desert of Judea; the shepherds were keeping night-watch over their flocks. An angel suddenly appeared to them and they found themselves surrounded by the "glory of the Lord," the accompaniment of a heavenly manifestation. Like Zechariah and Mary, the shepherds, too, were reassured: "Do not be afraid." The angel's message is a proclamation of good news and joy to all the people of Israel; for, despite the initial setting of the birth of Jesus in the framework of world history (2:1), the universalist note is not again struck in this episode (as it will be in 2:32) and the horizon closes on the Jewish world.

"This day"—the long-awaited day of Israel's salvation— has dawned; a new-born child is the Savior who brings salvation. The Savior is "Christ the Lord": a messiah endowed with authority. It is he, not Augustus, who is Savior and bringer of peace. "For to you is born this day a savior who is Christ the Lord"—Luke has in mind Is 9:6, an oracle on the birth of an heir to David's throne: "for to us a child is born, to us a son is given," bearing the fulsome titles: Wonderful, Counselor, Divine Hero, Everlasting Father, Prince of Peace. Luke has substituted the titles Savior, Messiah, Lord, current in christian tradition. Again like Zechariah and Mary, the shepherds are given a sign: "Let them go and see for themselves that they are not the victims of illusion; they shall find a child in a manger, not left naked and abandoned as they might expect to find a child who had been put in such an odd cradle, but properly clothed in swaddling bands."[3]

The presence of the "glory of the Lord" (v 9) had already assured the shepherds that something wonderful was afoot; now they hear the song of a heavenly choir—thus has Luke brought out the true dimension of a moment of simplicity.

[3]M-J Lagrange, *The Gospel of Jesus Christ* (London: Burns & Oates, 1938), 38.

Glory to God in the highest heavens and peace on earth to men
who enjoy his favor.

It appears that this canticle of the angels, like the Benedictus
and Magnificat, had come to Luke from a Jewish-Christian
milieu. It would seem that "Glory to God" expresses not so
much a wish ("let God be glorified") as a statement, a
recognition of the significance of the hour, an acknowledgment
of the saving deed of God. The familiar translation of *eudokias,*
peace to men "of good will," referring to human goodness, fails
to convey the true meaning; the renderings "with whom he is
pleased" and "who enjoy his favor," pointing to the divine
benevolence, suit the term and the context. In biblical
thought, God alone is the source of human goodness. The
sense of the angels' canticle is that, in the birth of the Messiah,
God is glorified, his power and his mercy are manifest, and, on
earth, the people whom he loves (people like Simeon and
Anna) receive the divine blessing of peace, the peace which the
Savior has brought.

The shepherds, informed by the angels of the birth of the
Savior, went in haste to verify what had been told them. They
found a scene which is etched on the imagination of
Christians: a stable, a manger with an infant child lying there,
a woman and a man watching over the child. And, having
feasted on the scene, they went away praising and glorifying
God for all they had seen and heard. Christ the Lord, they
now knew, was part of their world, Savior of the humble.
They, who had shown spontaneous trust in the heavenly
messenger, exemplify the spontaneous faith dear to Luke.
Naturally, they spoke freely of what they had seen and of the
things that had been told them, and their hearers wondered. In

contrast to the garrulous shepherds, Mary kept all these happenings to herself, treasuring them and pondering over them. For Luke, Mary is already the first christian believer (1:45) and will emerge so later (8:21; Acts 1:14). She is the one who believes, the handmaid of the Lord. In his customary manner, Luke winds up the episode by noting the return of the shepherds to their flocks. They went on their way "glorifying and praising God": joyful thanksgiving is a favorite theme of Luke.

The shepherds were not part of the religious establishment of the day and would be contemputuously regarded by establishment people as "that rabble that know not the Law" (Jn 7:49). In truth, they were people of faith who gladly heard the divine word and acted on it—their haste reflected their ready hearkening to the word. They "made known" what they had been told and what they had seen—they were the first preachers of the good news!

SIMEON (Lk 2:22-35)

In 2:22-34 Luke has combined two requirements of the Law: purification of the mother after childbirth and consecration of the first-born to the Lord. According to Lev 12:2-4, a mother was "purified" forty days after the birth of a son. Mary made the offering of the poor: a pair of birds (instead of a lamb). The "purification" regarded strictly ritual uncleanness and did not, of course, imply a moral fault in childbirth. If Luke has mentioned the purification of Mary it is because it happened to be associated with the presentation of Jesus in the Temple. The first-born son (he "that opens the womb") belonged to the Lord (Ex 13:2, 12) but was redeemed, bought back, by payment of a stipulated sum (Num 18:15-16). It is nowhere laid down in the law that the first-born should be taken to the Temple and presented there. But Bethlehem is a mere five miles from Jerusalem. And, besides, Luke needs to get child and parents to Jerusalem and the encounter with Simeon and Anna.

It was fitting that Jesus, already acknowledged by shepherds, should, on coming to the temple, be greeted by one of the Anawim, the "Poor Ones," who lived and manifested a distinctive feature of Jewish piety: they were those who did not trust in their own resources but relied in utter confidence upon God. Such a one was the righteous and devout Simeon who awaited, with faith and patience, the fulfillment of the hope of Israel, its consolation (cf. Is 40:1; 49:13; 51:12; 61:2). The Holy Spirit had assured him that he would not die until he had seen the Messiah. Now the Spirit had moved him to visit the Temple and had revealed to him that the infant who was at this moment being presented there was indeed the longed-for Messiah.

We have seen that the Matthean magi story displayed the magi reacting with acceptance and homage to the proclamation of the Messiah. Luke's shepherds play a similar role. But the magi story has two elements lacking in the Lucan story up to now: the positive response of Gentiles and the Jewish rejection of the new-born Messiah. These are supplied in Simeon's double oracle (2:19-32, 34-35). The *Nunc Dimittis* introduces the theme of salvation for the Gentiles (cf. Is 42:6; 52:10). He realized that, in view of the fulfillment of the promise made to him (v 26), death must be near; he can die in peace like Abraham (Gen 15:15) but more privileged than

Abraham. His cup was filled to overflowing because he had gazed upon the "salvation of God," the Messiah whom God had sent to save his people. And not the chosen people only: the Gentiles were destined for salvation. In this passage, for the first time in Luke's infancy gospel, we look explicitly (cf. Lk 2:1) beyond Jewish limits to a universalist horizon—salvation for all.

In the second oracle (2:34-35) Simeon anticipated the rejection of Jesus by the Jewish authorities and the rejection of the christian mission to Israel as described in Acts. Though this infant had come as the Savior of his people, he would be rejected by many of them, for he will stand as a sign of contradiction. He is the light that reveals the inmost thoughts; he is a sword of discrimination and a sword of testing (cf. Ezek 14:17). In face of him, "inmost thoughts," thoughts hostile to Jesus, will be mercilessly revealed. The parenthetical word to Mary—that the sword will pierce her heart—indicates that, as part of Israel, she, too, will be tested. But she will not fail.

ANNA (Lk 2:36-38)

After a prophet a prophetess—the delicate touch of Luke. Anna, now eighty-four, having lost her husband seven years after an early marriage, had chosen to remain a widow. She practically lived in the Temple, so uninterrupted were her prayers. A typical saint of Judaism, one of the Anawim, she is also an example to christian widows (cf. 1 Tim 5:5, 9). Her prophetic instict enabled her to recognize the infant Messiah and, gratefully, she spoke of him to those who, like Simeon and herself, looked for the salvation of Jerusalem (Is 52:9), that is, of Israel, God's people.

We welcome Anna for another reason. The New Testament writings are androcentric (male-centered) texts and women are on thin ground. Though we have come to learn that they are more present—present behind the term "disciple" for instance—than we had suspected, it is still gratifying to find a woman singled out for special mention. All the more when it is one of the caliber of Anna. A "little person" in her own estimation, she is great in the eyes of the Lord. She had been privileged to gaze upon the one who was the salvation of God: light to Gentiles and glory of Israel. And she, too, like the shepherds, was a preacher of the Good News. A lesson—a salutary lesson—of Luke's story is the declaration, exhilarating or disturbing according to one's thinking, that the first christian preaching was done by unlettered and despised shepherds and by an elderly widow.

WHAT THEN WILL THIS CHILD BE?

The gospel portrait of John the Baptist reflects the particular interest of each of the four evangelists. In Mark the Baptist appears on the scene right away (Mk 1:2-8) and solemnly proclaims the coming of the greater than he. The arrival of John himself had not been unprepared: he is the messenger (Mal 3:1) and the wilderness prophet (Is 40:30) foretold in the Scriptures. In the Fourth Gospel the Baptist goes out of his way to stress that he is no more than a witness to the Light (Jn 1:6-8), that he is subordinate to the Coming one (1:15). Explicitly, he is *not* the Messiah, *not* an Elijah come back to earth, *not* the prophet-like-Moses (1:19-23). He is the one who pointed to the Lamb of God (1:29, 36), the one who had seen the Spirit descend and abide on him who will baptize with Holy Spirit (1:30-33). Matthew and Luke offer a fuller treatment of the Baptist than does Mark and a much more positive evaluation of him than that of the fourth evangelist. Of the two, Luke has the more complete coverage.

Already in his infancy gospel Luke proleptically characterizes the Baptist yet to be born as an ascetic prophet summoning Israel to repent (Lk 1:15-17). At his birth the excited rumor ran through all the hill country of Judea: "What, then, will this child be?" (1:66). He will be prophet of the Most High proclaiming the ways of the Lord, pointing the way to forgiveness of sin and salvation (1:76-77).

Annunciation of the Birth of the Baptist (Lk 1:5-25).

The introduction (1:5-7) gives four items of information. The first three—time setting in the reign of Herod, the names Zechariah and Elizabeth, and their priestly descent—are items of tradition. The other, that they were aged and Elizabeth barren, reflects the stories of Abraham and Sarah (Gen 17:15-21), Elkanah and Hannah (1 Sam 1). Thus, the birth of John the Baptist is in continuity with the births of famous figures in the salvation history of Israel.

The pattern of annunciation (1:8-23) follows the pattern used to proclaim the birth of Ishmael (Gen 16), Isaac (Gen 17) and Samson (Judges 13) and carries echoes of Dan 8:16-17; 9:21-23. The Lucan angel is named Gabriel as in Daniel. The vv 15-17, which prophetically characterize the adult Baptist as an ascetic prophet calling upon Israel to repent, are culled from the ministry portrayal of him—3:1-3; 7:24-35. The sign, required by the literary pattern, is dumbness, suggested by Dan 10:15. Since Elizabeth's preganancy is going to be a sign for Mary (1:36) her seclusion (1:24-25) underlines its sign-value since no one could have known of her pregnancy. For Zechariah and Elizabeth, Luke has looked to the Old Testament models of Abraham and Sarah; for the infant Baptist he drew on the description of John in the gospel story of the ministry. He has portrayed the Baptist in conscious parallel to Jesus—taking consistent care to keep the latter on higher level.

The earnest prayer of a younger Zechariah was to be answered at an unexpectedly late date (Lk 1:13). Together with the promise God announced the name of the child: John—"Yahweh gives grace"; and John will indeed herald the age of grace. So it is that the natural joy of a father will be transformed into a greater joy and many will rejoice when, in due time, John will stand forth as the greatest of the prophets of Israel (cf. 7:26-28)—prophet in the stern cast of Amos. His characteristics and achievement are outlined in the angel's words.

Like the Nazirites (Num 6:23; Jg 13:4-5; 1 Sam 1:11) and the Rechabites (Jer 35), the notable ascetics of Israel, John will abstain from strong drink. He will be filled with the Holy Spirit "from his mother's womb." Here, as almost everywhere in the infancy narrative, the "Holy Spirit" is the spirit of prophecy and the meaning is that John is called to be a prophet from (or before) his birth, like Jeremiah (Jer 1:5) or the Servant of Yahweh (Is 49:1-5). It was widely believed (Mal 3:1; Sir 48:10-11; Mt 17:10; Jn 1:21) that the messianic era would be preceded by the return of Elijah; here it is shown that John is that Elijah-figure. The verse is a—rather free—quotation of Mal 3:23-24: John's preaching of repentance will leave the people well disposed for the coming of the Lord.

The birth of John (1:57-58) marked the fulfillment of the

angel's message to Zechariah. Circumcision was prescribed for the eighth day after birth. Elizabeth, to the consternation of relatives who had objected to her choice of name, was supported by her husband: the child's name was John. At that Zechariah found himself able to speak again. The infancy story of the Baptist closes (2:80) with a "refrain of growth" indicating his physical and spiritual development. In typical Lucan style, reference to John's sojourn in the desert prepares the way for his next appearance (3:2).

The *Benedictus* (1:68-79), like the *Magnificat* (1:46-55), was inserted, by Luke, into his original prose narrative. It is loosely appended to the account of the circumcision of John; if the canticle were removed, v 80 would fit smoothly after v 66. Like the Magnificat, this canticle is a chain of Old Testament quotations and reminiscences; it is a pre-existing psalm put, by Luke, in the mouth of Zechariah. The psalm celebrates the salvific intervention of God: the granting of the Messiah promised to David (vv 67-81), the peaceful possession of the land promised to the patriarchs (vv 72-75) and the light promised by the prophets (vv 78-79). The "rising sun" of this final stanza is the Messiah, not the Baptist, to whom the hymn was not primitively addressed. It was, originally, a christological hymn, reflecting very early christology. To adapt it to the new situation, Luke added the verses 76-78 which proclaim the mission of the infant precursor in terms that evoke at one and the same time the prophetic description of his adult mission (cf. Lk 3:4; 7:27), and the apostolic kerygma of the earliest church (cf. Acts 5:31; 10:43; 13:38; 16:17; 28:28).

The Baptist

How does one evaluate the Baptist? One is not likely to improve on Jesus' assessment of him: Lk 7:24-35 (Mt 11:7-

19). Jesus' testimony firmly relates John to God's plan of salvation. The rhetorical questions serve to define—in terms of what John was not—the role of the Baptist. John is no reed bending to every wind but a granite figure; he is no flaccid courtier but a prisoner of conscience in Herod's dungeon. He is indeed a prophet, a spokesman of God. For that matter, he is "more than a prophet" because as Elijah *redivivus* (Mal 3:1) he is precursor of Jesus and because no other, not even the prophets of old, is greater than he. The further statement— "yet he who is least in the kingdom of God is greater than he"—does not cancel the unique status of John. Rather, the contrast is between the age of promise and the age of fulfillment. It is quite like Heb 11. Following on a eulogy on the faith of the saints of Israel we read: "And all these, though well attested by their faith, did not receive what was promised" (11:39). In Jesus' judgment on his own generation who will listen neither to John nor to Jesus (7:31-35) the ascetic life-style of John is highlighted.

The baptism of Jesus by John is unquestionably historical. It could not have been invented by Christians. For that matter, Mt 3:13-15 shows manifest embarrassment. What becomes clear is that Jesus of Nazareth, hearing of the Baptist movement, came to see for himself and was impressed by what he saw and heard. John the Baptist was the only person in the society of his day who impressed Jesus. Though he admired John, Jesus followed his own path. John was a prophet of doom who preached a "baptism of repentance for the forgiveness of sins" (Mk 1:4). Jesus proclaimed; "the kingdom of God is at hand" (1:15). Where John had prophesied the judgment of God, Jesus prophesied the salvation of God. Hearing, in prison, of the activity of Jesus, a perplexed Baptist sent two of his disciples to enquire: "Are you he who is to come, or shall we look for another?" (Lk 7:19). And the answer was: "Go and tell John what you have seen and heard: the blind receive their sight, the lame walk, lepers are cleansed, and the deaf hear, the dead are raised up, the poor have the good news preached to them" (7:22). There is another prophetic message, another prophetic style.

In the infancy gospel Luke has taken care to keep Jesus one step above John. It was one step that made a world of difference, as he was fully aware. There is no doubt as to the greatness of John and his place in God's design. But his vision was not that of Jesus and his message lacked the warmth of the one who, from his place "in the bosom of the Father" (Jn 1:18), next to the heart of God, could and did speak of the foolish love of God. John suffered from the affliction of wholly dedicated persons with reforming passion: the temptation to impose *their* God, usually a humorless God. Characteristically, John lacked a sense of humor. Jesus did have a sense of humor—witness his outrageous parable of The Astute Steward (Lk 16:1-8). And we can hear a chuckle when he found himself trumped by the quickwitted woman (Mk 7:25-30). The Baptist is great, no doubt of that. But the greater than he had a message and a vision that transcend the Baptist's fondest dream.

꛷ ✳ ꛸

3

THE MOTHER

Because the purpose of the infancy gospels is mainly christological, it is self-evident that interest focuses on the Infant. Yet, we have seen that there are other actors whose role is surely not that of extras. There is one who stands out. Not so much in Matthew's story, let it be said. But, even in Matthew, Mary plays a not insignificant role. In Luke, Joseph is a stylised figure and Mary is, literally, the *prima donna*. It is no surprise, then, that this chapter will look mostly to Luke. Still, one begins with Matthew.

THE FIFTH WOMAN
(Mt 1:16, 18-25; 2:11; 2:13-15; 2:19-23)

Matthew's genealogy (1:1-17), we have seen, lists four women—"holy irregularities"—Tamar, Rahab, Ruth and Bathsheba. They prepare the way for the fifth woman, Mary, the holy irregularity *par excellence*. Throughout his genealogy Matthew employs a recurring formula: "A begot B," "B begot C," and so on. In v 16 one would have expected "Joseph begot Jesus." Instead, we find: "Joseph, the husband of Mary, of whom Jesus *was begotten."* The evangelist insinuates that, while Mary is surely the mother of Jesus, Joseph was not his father. Indeed, the fact left Matthew in something of a quandary: he has to show that Jesus is "son of David" (*despite* his virginal conception. The subsequent annunciation-to-Joseph episode (1:18-25) ends with Joseph formally acknowledging the Spirit-begotten; the *how* of Davidic sonship is through the agency of Joseph. Yet the child conceived through Holy Spirit is ultimately Emmanuel: God-with-us. "When Matthew tells us that Jesus, who through Joseph's acknowledgment is the descendant of the royal Davidic line, has been begotten in the womb of a virgin through God's Holy Spirit, he sees a very tight connection between Davidic and divine sonship. For Matthew it is a most literal fulfillment of the promise of God to David through Nathan: 'I shall raise up *your* son after you . . . I shall be his father, and he shall be *my son* [2 Sam 7:112, 14].' [1]

At the bidding of an angel, Joseph took his betrothed to his Bethlehem home. In stating that Joseph had no sexual relations with his wife before the birth of Jesus, Matthew, in view of the Isaian prophecy (v 23), wants to stress that Mary will give birth to her son while still a virgin. The "until" or "before' ("he knew her not until she had borne a son") does not, of itself, imply that Joseph and Mary had normal marital relations after the birth of Jesus. But the *text* does not exclude that possibility. The perpetual virginity of Mary is a post-biblical tradition, and not a biblical datum. At any rate, from now on, Mary is linked with husband and son. Interestingly, though, Joseph is not mentioned as being present when the

[1]Raymond E. Brown, *The Birth of the Messiah,* 137.

magi visited his home—"going into the house they saw the child with Mary his mother" (2:11). In the following episode Joseph is bidden to "take the child and his mother" first to Egypt and then back to Nazareth (2:13-23). Mary is thus associated with the symbolic journeys of her son. Like him, she too becomes part of the history of her people, part of the exile in Egypt and of the later exile in Babylon. It is Matthew's counterpart to Simeon's word: "and a sword will pierce through your own soul too" (Lk 2:35). Reference to Luke is appropriate; the rest of the chapter will be concerned with his story.

THE CHOSEN ONE (Lk 1:26-38)

Luke asserts the basic fact that Mary was called, and knew herself to be called, to be mother of the Messiah. It was, for her, a profound spiritual experience, a matter between herself and her God, something that took place in the depth of her being. In seeking to give expression to this personal, spiritual experience, Luke spontaneously turned to the Scriptures. He brings before us an angelic messenger: Gabriel, one of the "angels of the face" of Jewish tradition who stand in the immediate presence of God; and he provides the dialogue that brings out the significance of the call. The scene is set in Nazareth, a little Galilean village, an insignificant place ("Can anything good come out of Nazareth?" Jn 1:46), to a young girl of marriageable age. Indeed, Mary is already betrothed. In Jewish law betrothal was a valid and binding contract, but not until the groom had taken the bride to his home (Mt 1:24) did the couple live as man and wife. In the case of Mary and Joseph this final step was taken until after the visit to Elizabeth: from Judea Mary returned to *her* home (Lk 1:46). We have noted that, for Matthew, the home of Joseph and Mary was in Bethlehem. Though in Lk 1:27 the term *parthenos* ("virgin") need mean no more than that Mary was *still* a virgin, Luke's care to tell the reader twice that Mary was a virgin (1:27) is relevant, as we shall see, to the manner of Jesus' conception.

The structure of Lk 1:26-38, like that of 1:5-25 (annunciation of the birth of the Baptist), follows faithfully the Old Testament pattern of angelic annunciations of birth. Hence, material not explained by the literary pattern is significant: the peculiar manner of conception (virginal), the future accomplishments of the child (vv 32-33, 35), and the portrait of Mary in vv 34 and 38. "Hail, O favored one" (v 28)—the opening words of Gabriel are a greeting, but scarcely a concentional greeting. What is implied is that Mary has been chosen to play a unique role in God's plan; she is object of God's favor because of what is asked of her. And now, too, the statement, "the Lord is with you," falls into place. Once it is recognized that the title Favored One is functional, designating a divinely appointed role, then the assurance that the Lord will be with the chosen one is a guarantee of the effective accomplishment of the divine purpose.

In words reminiscent of the annunciation of the birth of Ishmael (Gen 16:11), Mary is told that she will be mother of a son whom she will name Jesus. In vv 32-33 this Jesus is described as the Davidic Messiah, in terms taken from 2 Sam 7:9-16. Luke uses the technique of Mary's question and Gabriel's answer (vv 34-35) to indicate the true identity of the Davidic Messiah: together they speak Luke's christological message. The Messiah is God's Son and his conception is not by way of marital intercourse (Mary) but through the Holy Spirit (Gabriel). It is Luke's graphic version of an early christological formula, such as that of Rom 1:3-4—"descended from David according to the flesh, and designated Son of God . . . by his resurrection from the dead."

Virginal conception is patently proposed by Matthew. Is it as clear in Luke? Yes, if the contrast of Baptist and Jesus is given due weight. John is "great before the Lord" (Lk 1:15a), Jesus is "great," without qualification (1:32a). John is "filled with the Holy Spirit from his mother's womb" (1:15), the very conception of Jesus involves the Holy Spirit that "comes upon" his mother (1:35). John will "make ready for the Lord a prepared people"(1:17), Jesus will rule over the house of Jacob-Israel and possess an eternal kingdom (1:33). John's conception is miraculous (1:7, 18). If the conception of Jesus were normal then the superiority of Jesus breaks down at a crucial point. But if the conception of Jesus is not only miraculous but virginal the careful pattern is preserved. It is noteworthy that just as Luke declares the age and barrenness in 1:7 and has Zechariah repeat it in 1:18, he describes Mary as a virgin in 1:27 and has her own attestation of it in 1:13. He thus draws our attention to his assertion of virginal conception.

All very well, but how is "virginal conception" to be understood? It is to be noted that in each infancy gospel the second chapter (Mt 2; Lk 2), read by itself, would not lead to the conclusion of a virginal conception. There is no echo of the claim elsewhere in the New Testament but it later became widely accepted in christian belief. One must endorse the need, in our day, of honestly seeking to grasp what the creedal formula *natus ex Maria virgine* really intends to say. Is it a *theologoumenon*, a theological statement—or does it necessarily demand biological virginity? What is not in doubt is that both Matthew and Luke are primarily interested in virginal conception as the expression of a christological insight that Jesus was God's son in a unique sense.

In accordance with the literary form of angelic message, Mary, like Gideon (Jg 6:17, 21) and like Zechariah (Lk 1:18-20), is given a sign, a guarantee of the authenticity of the message—though, in her case, the sign was unsolicited. Luke's v 37 is an almost verbatim quotation of God's words to Abraham in relation to the promised birth of Isaac (Gen 18:14). The portrait of Mary in 1:38—"Behold, I am the handmaid of the Lord; let it be to me according to your word"—is shaped from Luke's account of her in the ministry of Jesus (8:19-21). As one who hears and does the will of God she is truly handmaid of the Lord. In Mary's consent we discern Luke's estimation of her faithfulness. Now that she knows the divine purpose she accepts that purpose unhesitatingly and with perfect simplicity. If heroics would be out of place at such a moment so, no less certainly, would a protestation, even a suggestion, of unworthiness. Mary was too completely God's to think of herself at all.

On the basis of Mary's question in v 34—"how can this be, since I have no husband?"—some have asserted that Mary had made a vow of virginity or, at least, had come to understand that she was to remain a virgin. Such speculation is pointless: the question is not a question of Mary but a clever literary device of Luke. In the same vein, from v 38 we can deduce nothing of Mary's understanding of what was being asked of her. Her response is faith—total trust in God. Granted that, one may still wonder if she had really known who and what that promised child would be. The gospels make clear that even the Twelve came to understand who their Master was on the other side of resurrection. There is no reason to suppose that it was any different with Mary. We shall see that Elizabeth draws attention to her *faith*. She is one who lived by faith, who lived in the darkness that is an unavoidable feature of faith. And surely if Jesus, "like his brethren in every respect" (Heb 2:17), lived a fully human life, nothing less can be asked of his mother. Well-intentioned but unenlightened piety has not helped and does not serve the cause of christology and mariology.

Luke, writing in the light of his resurrection-faith, had discerned Mary's stature. She was mother, specially chosen, of Jesus—the Spirit-begotten. She was mother of a *unique* son— the one who would save his people from their sins. She was, truly, the most blessed of womankind (cf. 1:42).

THE WOMAN FOR OTHERS (Lk 1:39-56. [Jn 2:1-5])

In the structure of the Lucan infancy narrative this passage "The Visitation," is a complementary episode, a pendant to the diptych of annunciations (1:1-38). Elizabeth is granted the perception not only that Mary is with child but that her child is the Messiah. Her canticle in praise of Mary (1:42-45) echoes Old Testament motifs and anticipates motifs that will be found in the gospel (11:27-28). This narrative serves as a hinge between the two birth stories, of John and of Jesus. And this meeting of women illustrates their respective situations. Elizabeth's pregnancy was not only a sign for Mary; it was also an invitation. The "haste" of Mary was inspired by friendship and charity.

At Mary's greeting Elizabeth felt the infant stir within her—John, while still in the womb, is precursor (1:17) of the Lord. Enlightened by the prophetic Spirit she concluded that Mary is to be mother of "the Lord." That is why Mary is "blessed among women"—the most blessed of women. Elizabeth went on to praise Mary's unhesitating acquiescence of God's plan for her—her great faith: "And blessed is she who *believed* . . ."

> I have seen the Lord in her, but she is the mother of my Lord. My Lord is the one in whom she believes . . . Who am I that Mary, mother of my Lord, has visited me? I am the child of her believing in a child. I am the child of her love. Thus do I know Emmanuel: God is with us. Thus did I say, Blessed is she who has believed![2]

Mary's reply is her *Magnificat* (1:46-55). This hymn is the conclusion of, and the interpretation of, Luke's Visitation scene. In form a thanksgiving psalm, the Magnificat is a chain of Old Testament reminiscences and leans especially on the canticle of Hannah (1 Sam 2:1-10). There is no clear reference to the messianic birth—and this is surprising in view of the angel's message and the words of Elizabeth. Like the *Benedictus*, this psalm came to Luke from the circles of Jewish-Christian Anawim. The hymn originally referred to a general salvation through Jesus Christ. It will readily be seen that, without v 48, the *Magnificat* would fit smoothly in that Anawim setting. But we have the song in Luke's infancy gospel. There it stands between the Old Testament and the New and, like the rest of Luke's infancy narrative, captures the atmosphere of that

[2]Penny Livermore, *She Who Has Believed* (New York: Alba House 1968), lll.

unique moment. Luke presents the *Magnificat* as a canticle of Mary and we may, and should, read it as such.

Elizabeth had blessed Mary as mother of the Messiah; Mary gives the glory, in joyful thanksgiving, to the God who had blessed her, and through her, Israel: "My soul magnifies the Lord." The rest of the opening cry of joy (Lk 1:47) echoes the words of Habakkuk: "I will rejoice in the Lord, I will joy in the God of my salvation "(Hab 3:18). God had looked with favor upon his handmaid, upon her who is the most perfect of the "poor of Yahweh." Her total acceptance of God's will has won for her, the Favored One, everlasting glory. At once she turns the attention away from herself to the Almighty, the holy and merciful God, who has done great things for her. The Mighty One shows his power most of all in caring for the needy. In truth, the "steadfast love of the Lord is from everlasting to everlasting upon those who fear him" (Ps 103:17). All humankind will find hope in what God has achieved in Mary: loneliness turned into fruitfulness.

The interest then (vv 51-53) switches to Israel and to the manifestation of God's power, holiness and goodness in favor of his people. These verses are not concerned with the past, or not with the past only, but represent God' action at all times: what he has done to Mary and what he, through her as mother of the Messiah, has done for Israel, shows forth his manner of acting. He does mighty deeds with his arm, symbol of his power, when he reverses human situations—the proud, the mighty and the rich he has humbled and left empty, while he has lifted up and blessed with good things the poor of this world (the Anawim). This is nothing other than the message of the *Beatitudes* (Lk 6:20-21). For, if that message of Jesus were to bring abut the desired change of heart, the poor, the marginalized, would come into their own. It is God's "preferential option for the poor"—the option of a God who scrupulously respects human freedom. He awaits the response that will achieve the great transformation—but he looks for that response. The *Magnificat* anticipates Luke's concern, throughout his gospel, for the poor. It is echoed in Jesus' programmatic statement: " . . . the poor have the good news preached to them" (4:18).

The closing verses (54-55), in the mouth of Mary, point to the final intervention of God. His sending of the Messiah is the decisive act of his gracious treatment of Israel, the people which, through his covenant with Abraham (Gen 17:7), had become his "Servant" (Is 41:8-9). Mindful of his great mercy, he has fulfilled the promise made to the patriarch: a promise made to a man is accomplished in a woman.

Elizabeth had singled out Mary's faith for special attention and she had done so rightly. Still, there remains the more mundane, but refreshingly human factor that Mary had traveled from Nazareth to Judea to share the joy of her aged cousin and to lend a helping hand. One may refer to the Cana episode (Jn 2:1-15). True, it is a passage heavy with Johannine theology—and this is not the place to get involved in that aspect of the text. What matters here is that John has cast Mary as a charitable and practical woman who could be depended on to supervise, quietly but efficiently, a rural wedding. Each in his way, Luke and John have presented her as the woman for others. Not a surprise casting of her who is mother of "the man for others."

THE MOTHER (Lk 2:1-21)

While Matthew simply mentions the birth of Jesus (Mt 2:1), Luke lingers over it. Throughout the first chapter of his gospel, while dealing with the annunciations to Zechariah and Mary and with the birth of the Baptist, Luke's narrative has remained within the ambit of the Jewish world. Now, at the beginning of the second chapter, when he comes to the birth of him who is "a light for revelation to the Gentiles" (2:32) his perspective opens, if only for a moment, on to the Gentile world. His eyes have glanced from the Jerusalem of the beginning of his gospel to the Rome of the last chapter of Acts. The birth of the Savior of humankind is fixed—though perhaps too vaguely for our taste—on the calendar of world history.

The setting (2:1-7) is necessitated in part by Luke's assumption that Joseph and Mary lived in Nazareth before Jesus was born; for Matthew, their home was in Bethlehem. Luke has to get Mary to Bethlehem for the birth of Jesus there. His stratagem is the census of Quirinius and he is certainly confused in his account of the census—an unhistorical event as he relates it. But, then, it may be that we have tended to take Luke too literally. His prime interest would seem to lie in the fact that the mighty Augustus was, unwittingly, an instrument of the Lord. Through his decree it came to pass that Jesus the Messiah was born in the town of David. When we look at it dispassionately we must admit that what we had taken to be the Lucan picture of many distant descendants of David crowding into the insignificant Bethlehem is not very likely— still less likely as following on a policy of the practical Romans. What Luke wants to show is that Jesus was born in the city of

David as one who belonged there—not in lodgings like an alien. Manger and swaddling clothes (2:12) symbolize God's care and protection.

From the first, Mary is the caring mother, solicitously wrapping her baby and laying him in a manger-cradle. Luke is not suggesting anything miraculous about the birth—merely insisting that the "handmaid of the Lord" is, in her loving care, reflecting God's care. In the annunciation to the shepherds (2:8-14) heaven and earth touch. The angels interpret the event and give it its true meaning: this child is Savior, Messiah and Lord. The form of the proclamation (vv 10-11) and the canticle, the Gloria (2:14), would seem, again, to glance at Augustus who, architect of the *pax Augusta*, was hailed as Savior. Jesus, not he, Luke asserts, is Savior and bringer of peace.

In the reaction (2:15-20) to birth and heavenly proclamation the shepherds are forerunners of future believers who will glorify God for what they had heard and will praise God for what they had seen. In this third part of the passage all the protagonists, Mary, Joseph, baby and the shepherds come together. Yet, only one figure constitutes a bridge from the infancy narrative to the ministry of Jesus, and that is Mary, his mother. She is that by being a believer and disciple (Lk 8:19-21; 11:27-28; Acts 1:12-14). This is what Luke intends by his declaration: Mary "kept all these things, pondering them on her heart" (2:19). One should look to the parallel assertion in 2:51—"his mother kept all these things in her heart." She, like the Twelve, will come to full understanding when Jesus will have risen from the dead. Until then, in the obscurity of faith, she pondered those puzzling events. It is a misunderstanding of Luke's purpose, and of his literary achievement, to claim, as some have argued, that these statements point to Mary as source of the evangelist's narrative. Luke had access to some traditions but the infancy gospel, as we have it, is his creation.

The picture of Mary here is that of a loving and capable mother. Jesus was in very good hands. Furthermore she is a deep and thoughtful woman. And she is a woman of faith who lived her life in faith.

THE SUFFERING MOTHER (Lk 2:22-35)

As we have observed, in the setting of this episode Luke has combined two different Jewish customs: (1) consecration or presentation of the child to the Lord (Ex 13:1, 11-16); (2) purification of the mother after the birth of a child (Lev 12:1-8). Luke's text gives evidence of his general knowledge of these customs and of his inaccurate grasp of details. His real concern is with the witness of Simeon and Anna. Simeon's *Nunc Dimittis* introduces the theme of salvation for the Gentiles. Mary and Joseph were astonished at the glowing prophetic words. In the second oracle (2:34-35) Simeon anticipates the rejection of Jesus by the Jewish authorities and the rejection of the christian mission to Israel described in Acts. Here is where the mother is drawn into the destiny of her Son. He will be a "sign of contradiction," a challenge; the thoughts of those hostile to Jesus will come to light.

Mary stands among the smaller group of those who will "rise" rather than of those who will "fall." She, a daughter of Israel, will be tested like the rest. She cannot be different from her Son, the one who "in every respect has been tempted as we are" (Heb 4:15). Mary, too, will be tested and, like him, prove faithful. One thinks of John's scene of Mary at the foot of the cross (Jn 19:25-27)—a thoroughly symbolic scene. John has no intention of presenting a *mater dolorosa*. His intent, as at Cana (2:1-11), was to present Mary as representative of all those who seek true salvation.[3] Those who seek true salvation will meet with suffering. If the Son of Mary "learned obedience through what he suffered" (Heb 5:8), the mother, too, grew through what she endured. If John has Mary at the foot of the cross, one purpose of that is to suggest that she had, in the light of the resurrection, come to understand the meaning of the cross. Like Paul, she had come to see that the cross is God's definition of God and of humankind. The handmaid of the Lord, with her openness to God, could grasp the true meaning of the death of her Son. Her "pondering" had come to fruition.

THE BEWILDERED MOTHER (Lk 2:41-52)

The passage 2:41-52, concerning a twelve-year old Jesus, is hardly an *infancy* narrative, and the repeated conclusion, v 52 (cf. v 40), marks it as an addition. Originally, the story seems to have been a feature of the growth in awareness that what Jesus was recognized to be after the resurrection he was, in reality, still earlier. Here we have Jesus say of himself what the heavenly voice will say at baptism (Lk 3:22). Obviously, for Luke, the punchline is v 49. Jesus declares that his vocation

---

[3]Rudolf Schnackenburg, *The Gospel According to St John*, Vol. 3 (New York: Crossroad 1982), 274-282.

lies in the service of God who is his Father. By stressing Mary's lack of understanding (v 50) Luke makes the historically accurate assertion that the christology of Jesus as God's Son was not perceived until after the resurrection. "Luke is giving us a perceptive theological insight into history: there was a continuity from the infant Jesus to the boy Jesus to the Jesus of the ministry to the risen Jesus; and when christian disciples like Mary believed in Jesus as God's Son after the resurrection, they were finding adequate expression for institutions that had begun long before."[4]

Jesus' reply might be paraphrased: "Where would you expect a child to be but in his father's house?" The significance is that Jesus declares that God is his Father (in contrast to his legal father, v 48); he is conscious of a unique relationship to God. It is a relationship that he will voice by addressing his God as *Abba*. There can be no doubt of the fact that Jesus of Nazareth was conscious of a unique rapport with God. He was, and knew himself to be, "Son of God" at a level that none other of humankind could claim. It follows that the claims of his Father must override all other demands; his mission will break the natural ties of family (cf. Mk 3:31-35).

"Though the episode ends with the Lucan notice of his obedience to his earthly parents (2:51), his obedience as Son towards his heavenly Father transcends even that filial piety and obedience to Mary and Joseph. His independent conduct here strikes a chord that will be heard again in the Gospel proper. When the woman in the crowd praises Mary (11:27-28), he will offer a corrective that reveals that Mary has progressed, beyond the stage of misunderstanding attributed

[4]R.E. Brown, *op. cit.*, 494.

to her here (2:50), to that of one of those who hear the word of God and keep it. In other words, for Luke, Mary may be 'the mother of the Lord' (1:34), but it is much more important that her maternal ties yield to those of Jesus' heavenly Father. This is foreshadowed here."[5]

While all of this is so, one still needs to come to terms with Luke's Presentation story. Passover was one of the three pilgrimage feasts which, in theory at least, all adult Jewish men were obliged to attend. Women and children were not obliged, but women did freely accompany their husbands. Rabbinical ruling had it that a boy was not bound to make the pilgrimage before the completion of his thirteenth year, but it was customary for parents to take a boy with them at an earlier age. The setting, then, is vaguely credible, but the account will hardly stand up to close scrutiny. Let us be content with the story line. The boy Jesus went missing and was found "after three days," that is, on the third day, in the Temple. The relief of the parents was intense—"they were overcome"—and Mary's reproach was spontaneous expression of the pain she had suffered. In Luke's narrative Jesus does not offer much help. His juggling with the word "father" (vv 48-49) was unintelligible to Mary and Joseph. If the mother "kept all these things in her heart" she did so in bewilderment. There was no magic enlightenment. Her pondering in her heart prepared her for the day of understanding when, beyond death and resurrection, she stood as one of the believing community (Acts 1:14).

[5]Joseph A. Fitzmyer, *The Gospel According to Luke, I-IX*, (New York: Doubleday 1981), 438.

MARY

The Mary of Luke is a real, a warm, a thoroughly human person. She was faced with challenge; with decision. What young girl would not be taken aback at the assertion that *God* wanted her to be an unmarried mother! If Abraham is man of faith, Mary is surely woman of faith. As Abraham had spoken his "yes," Mary had spoken her *fiat.* As Abraham "went out, not knowing where he was to go" (Heb 11:8), Mary, with her "let it be to me according to your word" also handed God an open check. For Abraham "faith was reckoned to him as righteousness" (Rom 4)—the way, the only way, of standing right with God is by saying *yes;* is to let God be God *in his way.* Mary was one who said her "yes" to God.

4

THE STAR

Jesus

SON OF DAVID, SON OF ABRAHAM (Mt 1:1-17; 2:1-12)

We have seen that a main purpose of Matthew's genealogy was to present Jesus as "the son of David, the son of Abraham." This presentation of the Savior would appeal to the mixed Jewish-Gentile character of Matthew's community. The opening phrase, "the book of the genealogy of Jesus Christ," might be rendered "the birth record of Jesus Christ," and here "Christ" (= Messiah) has become a proper name. Jesus Christ is heir to the promises made to David and to the wider promises made to Abraham.

Son of Abraham

The implication of "son of David" will emerge in the titles and the formula-citations; the magi story delightfully brings out the meaning of "son of Abraham." As it stands (2:1-12) this is a self-contained story with no mention of Joseph nor of dream appearances. Matthew composed its sequel (2:16-18) when he combined it with the flight into Egypt episode (2:13-14). Unlike Luke, who describes the circumstances of the birth of Jesus, Matthew simply mentions it (2:1).

In the magi from the East, guided by the star (Num 234:17—"A star shall arise out of Jacob") in their search for a new-born "king of the Jews," and worshipping Jesus in Bethlehem (Mich 2:6), Matthew sees the Gentile world, attracted by the light of the Messiah, coming to pay homage to the "king of the Jews" in the city of David. The homage is described with the help of the scriptural theme of the kings of Arabia bringing their gifts to the King Messiah (Is 60:1-6; Ps 72-10-11, 15). Though, in fact, Jesus confined his ministry to Israel—"I was sent only to the lost sheep of the house of Israel" (15:24)—Matthew's gospel ends with a solemn commission of the Risen One: "Go therefore and make disciples of all nations" (28:19). The infancy gospels— remember they are primarily christological—make the point that what Jesus was and what, as Risen Lord he was seen to be, was (with hindsight) always true of him. That is why it is pointless to worry about "real magi" and a "real" star. The truth of the story is that Jesus *is* Savior of Gentiles. That is the "gospel truth."

Son of David

For Matthew, Jesus the Messiah is representative of God's people and, in his life, relives the history of Israel. The evangelist has set out to answer the double question: *Who* is Jesus and *how* has he come into the world? (ch 1). *Whence* did he come and *where* was he born? (ch 2).

Matthew's genealogy does not seek to *prove* the Davidic descent of Jesus; it has, rather, the theological intent of situating him within the divine plan of salvation: he emerges as the heir and as the fulfillment of God's purpose. The passage 1:18-24 (the annunciation to Joseph) answers the question raised by v 16 of the genealogy ("Joseph, the husband of Mary, of whom Jesus was born, who is called Christ".) It makes two points: that Jesus was virginally conceived and that Joseph, divinely enlightened, accepted the role of legal father of the child. In this manner Jesus is truly "son of David." Having thus presented the Messiah, Matthew goes on to depict his mission in an aura of light and of suffering. In anecdotic form he conveys what Luke has done through the mouth of Simeon (Lk 2:34-35—"this child is set for the fall and rising of many"): the call of the pagans to salvation (the magi); crisis and rejection in Israel (massacre of the innocents, flight into Egypt, obscurity in Nazareth.) All of these episodes are centered in biblical texts which bring out their theological significance.

Formula Citations

A feature of Matthew's gospel is his use of "formula citations"—Scripture quotations introduced by a fulfillment formula—which sit loosely in their context. They are particularly frequent in his infancy narrative: 1:22-23; 2:5-6; 2:15; 2:17-18; 2:23. The evangelist has recognized the applicability of particular Old Testament texts to particular incidents in Jesus' career. He introduced them because they fit his theology of the oneness of God's plan and because they help bring out, for his mixed christian community of Jews and Gentiles, who and what Jesus is. Let us look at the citations.

The first of them, 1:22-23, tells us that the virginally-conceived Jesus is Emmanuel, that he is *God-with-us*. The

significance of the name surfaces in the solemn assurance at
the close of the gospel: "Lo, I am with you always" (28:20). As
son of David he was, fittingly, born in Bethlehem (2:5-6). The
Hosea passage—"Out of Egypt have I called my son"
(2:15)—referred to the Exodus of Israel from Egypt. Matthew
sees that Jesus relives, symbolically, the history of his people.
Jesus is the Son *par excellence* truly meriting the title "son"
already given to Israel. In calling him from the land of exile,
God calls together with him the messianic people of which he
is the inclusive representative (Mt 1:1-17). His return is the
divine guarantee of the deliverance many times promised.

The story line in 2:16-18, involving he massacre of the male
children in Bethlehem, echoes Pharaoh's decree against the
male infants of the Hebrews. Matthew, with his formula
citation of Jer 3:15, works in another theme: that of the Exile
to Babylon. Again, Jesus is associated with a tragic event of his
people. The names in these three formula citations of chapter
2—Bethlehem (the city of David), Egypt (the land of the
Exodus) and Ramah (the mourning place of the Exile: Ramah
was the concentration camp where the deportees were
gathered for deportation to Babylon) are theologically sugges-
tive. The final episode (2:19-23) also gives us three significant
names: Israel, Galilee and Nazareth. The "citation" here is
really not such: Matthew is playing on the name Nazareth.
Quite likely, he is thinking both of the *neser*, "branch," of Is
11:1 and of *nazir*—one consecrated or made holy to God.
Jesus, he seems to say, is antitype of the Remnant come back
from Exile in humble circumstances, yet hope of messianic
salvation. At any rate, he knows that this son of David, Son of
God, is none other than Jesus the Nazarene.

In all of this one has to take seriously the subtle theological intent of Matthew. Luke's infancy story leaves no room for a "Flight into Egypt." Directly after the presentation of Jesus—that is, forty days after his birth—Mary, Joseph and baby returned to Galilee, to "their own city, Nazareth" (Lk 2:39). The question to be put to Matthew's narrative is: what does it mean? If one hears the right answer to the right question it is an answer rich in meaning. If one persists in putting the wrong question, one will miss the message and raise a host of false and distracting problems.

What is the message? I believe that the following statement puts it admirably:

"As Matthew narrates the infancy narrative, it is the place where the Old Testment and the Gospel meet. If he brought forward some themes from the Old Testament with which to clothe the infant Jesus, he also brought back from the Gospel some evaluations of Jesus by the Christian community: son of David, son of Abraham, and messianic Son of God. He attaches the basic Gospel revelation, 'You are the Christ, the Son of the living God' (16:16), to the conception of Jesus. He has this revelation proclaimed to Gentiles and Jews, to be received by the former and rejected by the authorities among the latter." [1]

[1]Raymond E. Brown, *The Birth of the Messiah* (New York: Doubleday, 1977), 231.

The Child

THE TITLES

The infancy gospel of Luke, no less than that of Matthew, is firmly christological. In Lk 1:31 May is told that she is to be mother of a son named Jesus—"who will save his people from their sins" (Mt 1:21). In Lk 1:32-33 Jesus is described as the Davidic Messiah in terms taken from 2 Sam 7:9-16. The only specifically christian trait here is that Jesus has been identified as the promised Messiah. Luke uses the technique of Mary's question and Gabriel's answer (1:34-35) to point to the true identity of Jesus: he is son of David and Son of God. It is Luke's dramatic version of an early christological formula such as that of Rom 1:3-4. Later christian formulaton will have it that Jesus is "true God and true man." All very well, if one understands what that language is trying to say. At least, in the setting of the Christmas story, one is not, even in the face of mystery, likely to lose hold on the humanness of this Son of Man.

We have noted that the Matthean magi story displayed the magi as reacting with acceptance and homage to the proclamation of the Messiah. But the magi story has two elements missing in the Lucan story up to now: the positive response of Gentiles and the rejection of the new-born Messiah. These are supplied in Simeon's double oracle (2:29-32, 34-35). Simeon can die in peace like Abraham (Gen 15:125) but more privileged than Abraham. His cup is overflowing because he has gazed upon the "salvation of God," the Messiah whom God has sent to save his people. And not his own people only:

the Gentiles too are destined for salvation (2:29-32; cf. Is 52:10; 42:6; 49:6). This messianic salvation is not only a beacon which shines before the nations, it s a brightness which dissipates their darkness and enlightens them. In his way Luke has made the point that the son of David is also son of Abraham. Significantly, in his genealogy (3:23-38), working backwards, he has Jesus as "the son of Adam, the Son of God" (3:38).

In the Septuagint Kyrios is the translation of *Adonai*, the reverential substitute for the name Yahweh. In Luke's infancy gospel "Lord" normally refers to God; but, twice, Jesus is meant (1:43; 2:11). Elizabeth greeted Mary as "the mother of my Lord"—that is, mother of the Messiah. In 20:41-44 and Acts 2:34 Luke uses Ps 110:1—"the Lord said to my Lord" to show that Jesus is Messiah and Son of God.

In 2:11 the angelic spokesman proclaims that "this day"— the long-awaited day of Israel's salvation—has dawned: a new-born child is the Savior who has brought salvation. *Sōtēr* is used of Jesus only here in the synoptic gospels, but it is used again by Luke in Acts 5:31; 13:23. This Savior is "Christ the Lord"—the title *Christos Kyrios* occurs nowhere else in the New Testament: he is the Messiah endowed with lordship and dominion (cf. Is 9:5). However, it would seem that Luke, in the context of the angelic message and the presence of divine glory (2:8-14) intends something more; and the figure of Augustus has relevance here too. "Lord," in the Septuagint a divine title, was, together with the title "Savior," claimed by the emperors (and other kings). By granting the title to this helpless infant, Luke is making his claim as to where true lordship is to be found.

In introducing his presentation episode Luke offers a rather free combination of Ex 13:2, 12—"Every male that opens the womb shall be called holy to the Lord". The word "holy" does not occur in the Exodus text; it has come from Luke who inserted the word also at 1:35—"therefore the child to be born shall be called holy." Its presence in the latter case is due to the influence of Dan 9:24—the consecration of a "Holy One" which will mark the inauguration of the messianic age—while its occurrence in 2:33 establishes a contact between Dan 9 and another messianic text, Malachi 3, for this last text stands behind Luke's description of the Presentation. Since in 1:16-17 and in the Benedictus Luke presents the Baptist as the messenger, the Elijah, who will prepare the way of Yahweh (Mal 3:1, 3), it must follow that the "Holy One" who is presented in the Temple is none other than the *Lord*: "Behold, I send my messenger to prepare the way before me, and the Lord whom you seek will suddenly come to his Temple" (Mal 3:1). In such a subtle and sophisticated manner does the evagelist propose his christology.

The fact is that Luke has a litany of christological titles in these chapters. The child is son of David; he is Messiah. He is Son of God in that he has a unique relationship to the Father. He is Lord—with overtones of the lordship of Yahweh; he is Savior. Luke uses this latter title once only in the gospel, in the word of the angel to the shepherds: "To you is born this day a Savior" (2:11). The title is not repeated, it is true, but it is noteworthy that the evangelist has drawn attention to the name given to the child at his circumcision—Jesus ["Yahweh saves"] (2:21). At any rate, the Christ of Luke is throughout, and before all else, a Savior who is full of compassion and tenderness and great forgiveness.

SIGN OF CONTRADICTION (Lk 2:33-35)

Though the infant has come as the Savior of his people he will be rejected by many of them. The point is well made in the Fourth Gospel: "He came to his own home, and his own people received him not" (Jn 1:11). He will stand as a sign of contradiction, a stone that can be a stumbling-block (Is 8:14-15) or cornerstone (Is 28:16) accordingly as people turn their backs on him or accept him (Lk 2:34-35). As usual, Luke is anticipating the reaction that Jesus encountered in his ministry: "Do you think that I have come to give peace on earth? No, I tell you, but rather division" (12:51). There is the reaction of his own Nazareth neighbors (4:16-30): "They rose up and put him out of the city, and led him to the brow of the hill on which their city was built, that they might throw him down headlong" (4:29). Luke has in mind, too, rejection of the christian mission to Israel, a recurring feature in Acts. It is enough to note the Lucan Paul's closing words to Israel (28:25-28) — "Let it be known to you then that this salvation of God has been sent to the Gentiles; they will listen" (v 28).

The child is set for the "fall and rising of many in Israel." There are two groups because Jesus is an abiding challenge. Again, the Johannine view is relevant. There can be no neutrality, for Jesus is the light that people cannot ignore (cf. Jn 9:39; 12:44, 50), the light that reveals their inmost thoughts and forces them to take part for him or against him. It is significant that "fall" is put first—sad recognition of the fact, lamented by Paul (Rom 9-11), that only a small part of Israel hearkened to the Good News. The sad truth is, Jesus will ever be a sign of contradiction.

THE HELPLESS ONE (Lk 2:7, 12, 16)

In his account of the birth of Jesus, manger and swaddling clothes are important for Luke—they symbolize God's care and protection. The splendor of angelic manifestation and heavenly glory at his birth was not reflected in the person of Jesus: he is the infant, lying helpless in a manger, a babe who will be circumcised on the eighth day (2:21). This contrast— between helplessness and splendor—can be seen to anticipate the death and resurrection of Jesus. One can look to the words of the risen Lord on the road to Emmaus: "Was it not necessary that the Christ should suffer these things and enter into his glory?" (24:26). The disciples, like the Jews in general, had not accepted *all* that the prophets had spoken (24:25); they had closed their eyes to the suffering of the Messiah (cf. 18:31; Acts 26:22-23). But, in God's design, the way to glory was the path of suffering (Lk 9:22; 22:69). Christ had suffered and so had already entered not his glory.

THE STRANGER (Lk 2:41-51)

Though the Finding-in-the Temple is only loosely connected with all that goes before, Luke has made a clever linkage. His infancy narrative proper closed with the "growth-saying" (v 40); the addition ends with another "growth-saying" (v 52). Though loosely attached, the passage neatly fits Luke's gospel plan. He has his gospel begin (1:5-23) and end (24:52) in the Temple; it suits his purpose to have his introduction, the infancy gospel, close with a Temple episode. Indeed, there is another factor. A distinctive feature of the

Gospel is the journey of Jesus from Galilee to Jerusalem (9:51—19:27). Appropriately, in 2:41-45, we have the boy Jesus already journeying from Galilee to Jerusalem.

The story has a twelve-year old Jesus make a statement about his relationship to his heavenly Father. That his place is in his "Father's house" means that his calling lies in the service of God. As usual, the boy is anticipating the declaration of the man: "My mother and my brothers are those who hear the word of God and do it" (8:21). Then, as now, he is not at the beck of his natural family. Still, he went down to Nazareth "and was obedient to them" (v 51). Luke's christology is sophisticated. He could, by assimilating this story, affirm that the boy Jesus was already consciously God's Son. At the same time he could assert that who and what he was did not become apparent until much later. Not only that—Luke is careful to stress the gradual growth in Mary's awareness. She finally understood when she had taken her place among the little circle of believers after Jesus' death and resurrection (Acts 1:14). And we, sharing her faith, have come to realize that Jesus, though wholly one of us, is always something more— though never less human than we.

LIKE US IN EVERY RESPECT (Lk 2:21, 22-24, 39-40, 52)

The Letter to the Hebrews presents Jesus as a Son who "had to be made like his brethren in every respect" (2:17), a Son who "in every respect has been tempted as we are, yet without sinning" (2:17). He is the human being who stands in a relationship of obedient faithfulness towards God (3:16) and who stands in solidarity with human suffering. Thereby he is mediator: a true priest who can bring humankind to God. If he bears "the very stamp of God's nature" (1:3) it is because we see in him what makes God God; he shows us that God is God of humankind. He had come to do the saving will of the Father and had learned God's purpose in the "school of suffering" (5:8). In Gethesemane he had prayed "with loud cries and tears to him who was able to save him from death" (5:7); he came to understand that the way of faithfulness led to the cross. Jesus , in his life and fate, lived the truth of Simeon's word—he was indeed a sign of contradiction.

This emphasis, by a christian theologian, on the humanness of Jesus was timely in its day and is no less timely in our day. Jesus shared our human condition; he can identify with us in our living and suffering and dying. His life shows us what true humanness is. And we must not be put off by reference to his sinfulness (4:15). That might be taken in one of two ways: *non posse peccare* (unable to sin) or *posse not peccare* (able not to sin). It surely has to be taken in the second sense. And this, too, is the meaning of Paul's statement: Christ "died to sin" (Rom 6:10)—he died rather than sin. Jesus gives us hope in our weakness because he experienced our human lot. He gives us comfort in suffering, for in and through his suffering he showed us that God is not aloof from our suffering. And, in death as in life, he bore witness to a loving God's limitless love of humankind.

We are not surprised to learn that what Jesus was throughout his adult life, he was from the start. If his conception was unique in that it was virginal, there was nothing remarkable about his birth. He came into the world with a cry, as every baby does. He had to be clothed and fed and cared for. He was "born of woman" (Gal 4:4)—he had entered fully into the human situation in all its vulnerability and weakness. Furthermore, "born under the Law," member of a pious and observant Jewish family, he was circumcised on the eighth day after birth (2; 210). It was a father's right to name his child and in this case too the heavenly Father had bestowed the name ("the name given by the angel before he was conceived in the womb," 2:21). The name Jesus ("Yahweh saves") suits perfectly the character of this Savior revealed to the shepherds, he who is Christ the Lord. For, there always is the other side to this one like us. And, indeed, a purpose of the infancy gospels is to remind us of that "other side."

As one "born under the law" Jesus was presented in the Temple forty days after birth (2:22-24). He accompanied his pious parents to Jerusalem for Passover (2:41-42). As a faithful Jewish boy he was obedient to his parents (2:51). Like any normal child, he developed physically and intellectually. The refrain of growth—"And the child grew and became strong, filled with wisdom; and the favor of God was upon him" (v 40) said of the baby being reared in his Nazareth home, is echoed in v 52 when the twelve-year-old had returned to his home: "And Jesus increased in wisdom and stature, and in favor with God and man." Both saying repeat in part what was said of the Baptist: "And the child grew and became strong in spirit." The saying of v 52 is practically a citation of 1 Sam 2:26—"Now the boy Samuel continued to grow both in stature and in favor with the Lord and with men."

Luke has carefully marked the physical development of Jesus: *to brephos,* "the baby" (2:16), *to paidion,* "the child" (v 40), *Iēsous ho pais,* "the boy Jesus" (v 43), *Iēsous* (v 52). In this latter verse we learn that his understanding too deepened and matured. The authentic humanity of Jesus demanded such growth in understanding. It also set limits to his knowledge. Here Scripture is formal (cf. Heb 2:17; 4:15; 5:7; Mk 13:32; 14:35-36). In short, Jesus would have blended with his Nazareth background. One can appreciate the amazed reaction when he first displayed his wisdom in his local synagogue: "Is not this Joseph's son?!" (4:22).

JESUS

In treating of Jesus it does not seem to make sense to end, as I might seem to have ended, on the key: "The Stranger." I have ended so quite deliberately, because I want to make two points. The first is that Jesus, though wholly one of us, is still apart from us. He is the human person who is unique. I contend that the evangelists Matthew and Luke have given an eminently well-balanced christology; in their infancy gospels the unique humanness of Jesus is manifest. My second point is that, unhappily, later christologies have made it difficult, if not impossible, to discern a truly human Jesus. Perhaps the secret is that Matthew and Luke (and Paul, too) know nothing of pre-existence. The question is: what does pre-existence (a non-biblical term) mean? For my part, I am content to go along with the Pauline statement: "God was in Christ, reconciling the world to himself" (2 Cor 5:19). That is the New Testament message: where Jesus is, there is the Savior-God.

But, then, one must be daringly logical—and traditional christology had suffered a failure of nerve. If God is in Christ—and that surely *is* christology—then we meet God in the manger, at the circumcision, in contradiction . . . and therefore on the cross. The infancy gospels teach us, in their way, what Paul and Mark teach, that we must let God be God. A manger is as foolish as the cross. But in the one, as in the other, we meet the true wisdom of God. At the beginning, as at the end, we meet helplessness: a new-born babe imprisoned in tight swaddling-bands, and that child, now a man, nailed helplessly to a cross. In the swaddled baby and in the crucified man God is challenging us to acknowledge *him* as the God who thrives in weakness, and to recognize ourselves in *the* human person who was wholly open to that weakness which is the only strength. There is no authentic Jesus other than the Jesus of the New Testament—and that authentic Jesus is really present in the "mini-gospels" of Matthew and Luke.

5

THE PEOPLE WE ARE

We have looked at the varied characters of our Christmas stories. I have endeavoured, in each case, to indicate some distinctive trait or traits; throughout, I have had this chapter in sight. I believe that the people of Matthew and Luke are fascinating. And all of them are distinctively human. We ought, then, to be able to recognise something of ourselves in them. In the last resort this will be achieved by each of us for herself or himself. It has seemed to me, however, that it would be helpful to provide some headlines. You may not be sympathetic to a characteristic I have discerned; or you may notice a trait I have missed. That is fine. My hope is that I will have pointed you to a dimension of the infancy gospels you may not have observed—to be honest, a dimension that I, too, had not formerly noticed. It is my experience that this approach has opened up a rich aspect of these stories. I try, as well as I can, to share my experience.

Abraham—The Man of Faith

Few of us will ever be challenged as Abraham was. Leave everything and go—later on I will show you where you are to go! Though old and childless you will be father of a countless progeny. You will sacrifice to the Lord the miracle child, the sole hope of promise fulfillment. What kind of God is this?— surely a contradiction. He makes unreasonable demands, makes impossible promises. And, having showed that he can deliver—hey presto!—he seems ready to destroy all again. Who can have faith in such a God? Well, Abraham put his trust in him. I become more and more convinced, not only that Abraham was right, but of why he was right. Abraham saw what Paul was to recognise, that his God is always a foolish God—a God who loves with divine abandon. He is not a God of calm reason, of cold logic. He is a warm-blooded God who dares to be unpredictible. He can make outrageous demands because he will always be faithful. Abraham could and did put his trust in this God because he was sure, as Paul was to be sure, that "the gifts and the call of God are irrevocable" (Rom 11:29).

What of Abraham himself? His basic faith is unquestionable. There were some hiccups, though. He had laughed a skeptical laugh at the announcement of the promise. He was to put that promise in jeopardy when, to save his own skin, he let Sarai be taken into Pharaoh's harem—"she is my sister." Later, he worked out, to his own satisfaction, how the promise might be fulfilled—through the surrogate motherhood of Hagar.

Abraham reminds us that greatness and frailty can coexist in the same human person; he sets a pattern that will be repeated in many of our characters. It is normal that our faith should have shades of doubt; we might do well to beware to the person who has no doubt at all. Do we not seek, in some measure, to avoid risks to ourselves—even at the price of another's risk? And do we not, readily enough, figure out how God wants us to act—in ways that make sense to us? I do not share the greatness of Abraham, but I am at home with him in his weakness!

Jacob—The Man of Guile

I believe that Hosea has said it all. In his heartening eleventh chapter, where he casts Yahweh as doting father of a first-born son, he has that Father declare: "I am God and not man" (Hos 11:9). What he means, in context, is that, if I were human, I would have run out of love long before now—but I am *God* . . . He is the God who knows every quirk of his human children. He may not be happy about our stupidity, our selfishness—even our sheer perversity. But he is not dismayed. He can and does make use of the most unpromising human material. Jacob is a case in point. Not an attractive character by any standard. He is the archetypical con-man. On at least three occasions he outwitted his pedestrian brother Esau. He had no scruple, and little difficulty—aided and abetted by his unprincipled mother—in pulling he wool over the eyes of his senile father. His rascally uncle Laban was a more formidable opponent. Even there, though he lost a battle or two, Jacob won the war. Yet, through the unsavoury shenanigans, this Jacob was furthering God's saving purpose.

Jacob raises the question: where is God to be found? He is

surely not in the dark areas of hatred and cruelty and violence. I mean that these carry no trait of God; but God is never aloof to any aspect of human suffering. The Jacob story carries the consoling message that God is in the grey areas of human connivance and self-interest. The Jacob story tells us that God takes us as we are. He smiles at our "wisdom," because our wisdom can serve his "folly." Jacob lives by his wits, manipulates people, is a successful "operator." The irony of his story is that, in a strange way, he does measure up to his role and status. That is most poignant in his grief for his lost son (Joseph) and for the sons he feared would be lost (Simeon, Benjamin) [Gen 37:34-35; 42:36]. In spite of his earthiness he can still mirror something of a God "who did not spare his own Son"—a God who grieved over the murder of his Son. If Jacob served God's purpose he was no human pawn. His grief is his redeeming feature because it joined him with a caring, grieving God.

If I see myself in Jacob all is not lost. The tragedy is for one who, having characteristics of Jacob, does not recognise them. Most of us, in some measure, can be unscrupulous in our selfishness. We can, and do, take advantage of those who are not as bright as we; we capitalize on the needs of others. The story of Jacob and Laban illustrates sharp practice in business. Even for professed Christians, business ethics are not always the ethic of the gospel. We are readily tempted by the "fast buck." I may smile at Jacob. But it should be a wry smile if I can admit that his conduct is not all that foreign to myself.

The Resolute Women

In his genealogy Matthew has included four strange but resolute women. They are links in the ancestry of the special son of Abraham and of David. For that reason and because of some irregularity in their marital relations, they are foils to Mary. Yet, they stand out in their own right. As human persons they lived their lives, coping with real, often painful, circumstances. They are not coventional saints. But each, in her way, is a challenge to us.

Tamar had been hard done by her father-in-law who would deprive her of her legal right. Her claim was not selfish: she was upholding the cause of her dead husband. She took the law into her own hands. In the event, Judah has to admit: "She is more righteous than I" (Gen 38:26). To see in Tamar's conduct an example of the end justifying the means is, for us, an obvious temptation—and a glaring instance of missing the point of biblical story. It is obvious that, in its context, her conduct is admirable: she was a woman of her day and age. She has done no more than the exploited widow of Jesus' parable: she had, in the face of male callousness, taken a womanly way to get her way (cf. Lk 18:2-5). A message is that the little ones of this world, the marginalized, have a God-given right to vindicate their rights. Is it not, after all, the message of the *Magnificat*?

Rahab and Ruth are less easy to assess. In the genealogy Rahab appears as wife of Salmon and mother of Boaz. She is certainly the Rahab of Joshua 2—she who had sheltered Joshua's spies. A snag is that Boaz comes nearly two centuries later than the age of Joshua; a marriage of Rahab and Salmon is unlikely, to put it mildly! Straightway, for us, a problem.

Biblical writers would shrug and ask: "What problem?" They put their question, not ours. Rahab was a woman who had read the writing on the wall. Jericho was doomed—she cut her losses and threw in her lot with the eventual conquerors. Not very noble, perhaps, but surely very human.

Ruth, a Moabitess, having lost her Israelite husband, elected to stick with her mother-in-law, Naomi. The shrewd older woman was able to engineer a marriage for Ruth with Boaz, kinsman of her late husband. Boaz emerges as a thoroughly honorable man. There is more than a suggestion that he was cleverly manipulated by the women. But all turned out well. Ruth, the Moabitess, became great-grandmother of David. Ruth is a touching human story. As in the case of Tamar there is concern for the right of a dead husband. There is, in Naomi and Ruth, and edifying love bond between mother-in-law and daughter-in-law. And there is the charming touch to the wiles of women: two admirable women who do, gently, manipulate an admirable man.

Bathsheba—"the wife of Uriah"—is rather different. It is easy enough to see that she was not notably upset at having caught the attention of king David. And there is no evidence of overwhelming grief at the death of her husband. Indeed, her major role in winning the throne for her son Solomon, and his obvious acknowledgement of her part, make clear that she was an ambitious woman. She is, in my view, the least attractive of the four.

There we have them. Now, what of us? We can ask ourselves if we have anything like Tamar's passion for justice. Rahab might alert us to a temptation to cut our losses. True, she had ended up on the winning side—but could she really live with herself? The love of the older and the younger women, Naomi and Ruth, of different nationalities, is surely a headline. And there is the message that romance, and a dash of female wiles, are precious human values. We should be grateful that we have the gift of the Song of Songs, that celebration of sexual love. There is the less savoury but no less human side. The love-affair of David and Bathsheba led to the callous murder of an innocent Uriah. We are joyously reminded that human love, when it is truly such, is God's loveliest gift to humankind. We are painfully reminded that we humans can pervert love. It seems to me that the four women are, in diverse ways, a radical challenge to all of us. They are a challenge to what can be best and what might be worst in our humanness.

David—The Flawed Saint

It could be argued that David is the most fascinating character in the whole of the Old Testament. Of course, he has had the inestimable advantage of having had a brilliant biographer. David, a real-life figure, simply steps from the pages of 1-2 Samuel. He is the erstwhile shepherd who slew an enemy champion and a talented musician who could soothe his troubled king. We learn of David's warm friendship with Jonathan, Saul's son, and his love for Michal, Saul's daughter. There is the paranoid pursuit of him by Saul—and then David's grief at the tragic death of Saul and Jonathan. Next, bitter civil war between Judah and Israel, ending with David having himself proclaimed king of a united kingdom of Judah and Israel. And his master-stroke, his establishment of Jerusalem—the city of David—as his personal capital, and the making of it the religious center of his kingdom.

David was a complex character who could be magnanimous and cruel. He was capable not only of adultery but of a calculated cover-up murder. Yet, he fasted and prayed for the life of a stricken child. He indulged his sons to the extent that he would become, not once but twice, target of their ambition. At the end, he had to let others bring about what he decreed. With all his faults, he remains a hero of God's people. It was he who established Zion as religious center of Israel. As traditional author of the Psalms he remains an architect of Israel's cultic heritage. It was he who heard the promise that his kingdom would not end. It was a promise fulfilled—beyond the expectation and the understanding of David—in the son of David, the Son of God.

I have named David "the flawed saint." What saint has not been flawed? Heroic virtue in one age can seem folly in another. Saints, attractive perhaps in their day, may seem repulsive in another time. Not that I suggest that David might ever look repulsive—he was too honestly human for that. He had human faults as well as human virtues. The comforting word of his life is that if one can rise, and then fall—one can rise again. David was a man who had the decency to admit his sin, a man who learned from his tragic experience. He was a man who loved not wisely but too well, loved women and his sons. He proclaims that it is better to love unwisely than not to love at all. In his way, he mirrored the foolish love of his God—and of his Son.

People of the Exile

Jeremiah and Ezekiel document the deplorable religious situation in Judah just before and during the Babylonian incursion that was to lead to the historical end of the house of David. In 587 B.C. not only the monarchy but Jerusalem and the Temple too went down in ruins. Where now was the promise to Abraham? Where now was the assurance to David that his kingdom would last forever? The trauma of the Exile dramatically underlined the fragility of a neat theological system and, thus, challenges the abiding validity of any theological system.

David, his days of flight and brigandage ended (forced on him by a paranoid Saul), became king, first of Judah, and then of the united kingdom of Judah and Israel. He had won for himself the city of Jerusalem and had made it his capital (2 Sam 5). By installing the ark of Yahweh there he turned it into the religious center of his domain. Then, adverting to the incongruity that he had a palace while the ark of Yahweh was still housed in a tent, he planned to build a *house* (temple) for Yahweh; instead, it was Yahweh who would build a *house* (dynasty) for David (7:4-17). "And your house and your kingdom shall be made sure for ever before me; your throne shall be established forever" (7:16).

In Judah this promise to David, the Davidic convenant, was to replace that of Sinai. Hope for the future rested in the Davidic line. The king of Judah was "Son of God" (2 Sam 7:14). No enemy could destroy the holy city and the blessed dynasty. This conviction was the theological basis of the hope of the eighth-century prophet Isaiah-ben-Amoz in the face of seemingly inevitable disaster. On the strength of that hope he was able to sustain his king, Hezekiah, when faced with an Assyrian threat (2 Kgs 19:32-35). A century after him, when Judah was threatened by Babylon, the prophet Jeremiah faced an impossible task in striving to convince his contemporaries that Nebuchadnezzar, unlike Sennacherib, would have his way and that Zion and its temple would perish. He was not believed. What Yahweh had done in the days of Hezekiah, he would surely continue to do. The son of David was son of Yahweh; Zion was city of Yahweh; the temple was his dwelling-place. A young Jeremiah would have adhered to that theology, the comforting theology of a promissary covenant. An older Jeremiah, faced with the patent failure of the Davidic monarchy, looked back to the Sinai covenant. What he was sure of, in the teeth of disaster, was that Yahweh could and would pick up the pieces and put them together again. Yahweh could do what "all the king's horses and all the king's men" could not do.

For Isaiah the traditional theology could still work, could still make sense. For Jeremiah, not in a very different situation, it no longer made sense. He had to look for another theology, one that really met his situation. Isaiah had looked for an Immanuel, the ideal Davidic king. He would never have recognized that future king in a helpless victim on a cross. One feels that Jeremiah might find him there. And Second Isaiah, with his Songs of the Suffering Servant, surely would. Isaiah (that eighth-century prophet), when put in perspective, alerts one to the fragility of any tidy theological system. God will not be confined. He must be allowed to surprise us. While our faith should grow in firmness, our theology should ever be open, open to the breath of the Spirit, alert to the "signs of the time." Today, we do not live in the age of Trent. We have witnessed the demise of neoscholasticism. We must fashion a theology—rather, theologies—for our day.

People After The Exile

Deuteronomy proposes a doctrine of the "two ways": the way of faithfulness to God and his commandments, the way of life; the way of infidelity, a way of death (Dt 30:15-20). In Judges this deuteronomic doctrine is illustrated in terms of a recurring cycle; infidelity—disaster—repentance—deliverance (Jg 2:6–3:6). The deuteronomists offered an explanation of the unparalleled disaster that was the destruction of Jerusalem and the Exile. The bottom had fallen out of Judah's world. Yahweh's promises to the patriarchs and to David had gone up in smoke. Was Yahweh a God incapable of protecting and sustaining his people? No. The key to the disaster was the fatal choice of the people: they had walked the way of death. It is not too late. They may still choose life; they may still get back on the right way. Repentance, *metanoia*, will, without fail, lead to deliverance and restoration.

The author of Is 40-55, an anonymous prophet of the Exile, is, for convenience, named Second Isaiah. We have no inkling of the identity of this man, one of the foremost poets and theologians of Israel. All that we do know is that he certainly belonged to the "Isaian school" and found his inspiration in the work of his eighth-century predecessor. He assumes that those he addresses had learned the deuteronomic lesson. They have come to their senses and have turned back to their God. They are poised for deliverance. He bends his evident poetic talent to the expression of his fervent conviction. There will be, unquestionably, a new Exodus. There will be a fresh flowering. The aftermath would show that the reality did not measure up to his expectation. But there was a change, irreversible. There was a return and a new phase of life for Judah. The enthusiasm he had drummed up was not sustained but he had started something, he had awakened his people to a new understanding of themselves and of their God. His universalist vision was an inspiration and a challenge.

The history of life in Judah in the centuries after the return was to show that, sadly, his vision was lost to sight. The community had found its way but, more and more, that way became *its* way. No longer was there gross infidelity. Instead, fidelity became an obsession. Faithfulness lay in meticulous observance of commandments, statutes and in ritual. It follows that God could no longer be, truly, a universal God. He could only be the God of those who served him according to the minutiae of Torah.

We are reminded of Vatican II and the post-conciliar Church. The Council, in the celebrated image of John XXIII, was an opening of windows, a letting the wind of the Spirit blow through. It was an opening of minds. There can be no going back. But there has been a hardening—there is no doubt of that. There is a certain yearning for a more secure but more closed Church.

Is security, then, the name of the game? Paul put the boot into the Galatians precisely because they were succumbing to a craving for security, the security of law—a surrogate conscience. Paul himself could declare: "Not that I have already obtained this or am already perfect; but I press on to make it my own, because Christ Jesus has made me his own" (Phil 3:12). Paul was confident of his place with Christ—but he was not complacent. He knew that, as a Christian, he ought to face up to responsibility. He had to make decisions and shoulder the risk of decision. Though he had no doubt about the rightness of his own basic decision to become a disciple of Christ, and though he had no doubt about his life with Christ beyond death (Phil 1:21-23), he knew that he still had to live with uncertainty. A case in point is his plan to visit Rome as a stage on his way to a mission in the virgin territory of Spain (Rom 15:21-23). He got to Rome alright, but surely not as he had planned. And there was to be no mission in Spain. It was not the only time Paul was to learn that "man proposes but God disposes."

To return to the post-exilic situation: what does one do when reality does not match up to the expectation? One can throw in the towel and bow to the "inevitable." The Christophers say: "Better to light a candle than curse the darkness." In the despondency of post-exilic gloom another prophet of the Isaian school—"Third Isaiah," author of Is 56-66—dared to hold aloft the torch of his starry-eyed predecessor. True, Second Isaiah seemed to be a romantic visionary who could and did cry out: "I have a dream!" Yet the prophets of doom are ever with us and are a sturdy breed. Third Isaiah, like Second Isaiah, reminds us of christian hope. It has always seemed to me that a pessimistic Christian is a contradiction in terms. Do we, or do we not, believe in the promise of our God? The wild exuberance of those prophets echoes the extravagance of their God. "Only God's wild laughter/could hope that things will turn out even" (Brendan Kennelly).

JOSEPH

Matthew assures us that Joseph was a "just man." He had lived, faithfully, according to the tenets of his Judaism. He was formally betrothed. He had taken the first, normally irrevocable, step into an honorable marriage with Mary. Then came the shock. This worthy man had to face the fact that his betrothed was pregnant—and he knew that he was not the father. He could never had dreamt that this could be true of Mary; but the evidence was unmistakable. One can picture his pain, his sense of betrayal. And yet, there was a lingering doubt: could there be some other explanation? Something had to be done, but he was torn between his reverence for the law and his concern for Mary. In desperation he decided to divorce her quietly. He probably never quite considered that this course of action would not help her at all. The only helpful way would have been to go ahead and formally marry the woman. But he was inhibited by his respect for law. His decision was not motivated by selfishness he just could not, in the long run, see himself free to do other than pursue the course he had worked out. He was trapped.

Then came enlightenment. And, once free, he did what, in his heart, he had always wanted to do. He did marry Mary and claim legal parenthood of her child. It must have been a mighty relief. He would have found it so hard to live with himself if he had followed through on his initial decision. From now on, in Matthew's story, he played a decisive and protective role.

Many of us find ourselves in predicaments not unlike that of Joseph. Law may indicate a course of action, but on the other hand stand persons and circumstances. How is one to act?—blindly to follow the law? or take the risk of following the heart? One should not forget the word of the Lord: "The sabbath was made for man, not man for the sabbath." Why should law always have the benefit of the doubt? And it is all too easy—again the word of Jesus (cf. Mk 7:1-13)—for man-made rules to become "law of God." At very least, the quite unhelpful "solution" of a perplexed Joseph might encourage us to trust in the Lord. No angel will whisper to us in our dreams. But the good news to Joseph may encourage us to take the risk of falling into the hands of God.

There is another aspect of the Joseph story that, sadly, can have poignant meaning for too many people. Joseph was a refugee, a displaced person. He was never to return to his Bethlehem home. Too many men, women and children throughout history, victims of war, of political expedience, of religious intolerance, have been made homeless. Too many have been exiled by economic stress and by other factors. The Matthean "holy family" holds hope for rootless people without hope. In the displaced persons, Joseph, Mary, Jesus, we have the assurance that God is with all displaced persons. Such misery, such suffering, is not of his willing. He will work no miracles because he has absolute respect for human freedom. He may seem uncaring, but he is never aloof from human pain—that is the message of the cross. Still, we need the lesson, too, of the homeless wanderer who is furthering the saving purpose of God.

HEROD

"When he heard that Archelaus reigned over Judea in place

of his father Herod, he was afraid to go there" (Mt 2:22). For Joseph, the shadow of Herod reached beyond his grave. Herod was a petty king of a petty kingdom, a king who ruled at the pleasure of Rome. He wielded power in his small domain and, likely, saw himself as a Caesar. He was, at the same time, a man with a gnawing sense of insecurity. Because of that, he was fiercely jealous of his power and paranoid in his suspicion of threats to his authority. In his insecurity and fear he could be provoked to irrational and ruthless action.

Collaboration of the ecclesiastical arm—the chief priests and scribes—reminds us of the ecclesiastical Herod, Caiaphas. His answer to the threat that, if Jesus were granted free scope, "the Romans will come and destroy both our holy place and our nation" (Jn 11:48), was that "it is expedient for you that one man should die for the people" (v 50). It is easy to read between the lines. Jesus was, by Caiaphas, perceived as a mortal threat: he had to go. Ecclesiastical power can be, in its way, as ruthless as civil power. It can be more ruthless because of its readily assumed sense of righteousness.

Herod stands as a salutary warning to all who wield authority. When hanging on to power becomes an obsession, then values are distorted and true morality goes out the window. Cruelty does not have to reach the obscenity of the "massacre of the innocents" to be cruelty. Too many spirits have been broken, too many lives have been destroyed by fearful people jealous of their need of power. Herod illustrates the wisdom of the *demand* of Jesus: "It shall not be so among you" (Mk 10:43).

Pointedly, he had prefaced his demand with the declaration: "You know that those who are supposed to rule over the Gentiles lord it over them, and their great men exercize authority over them" (v 42). He had, as unequivocally as is possible, ruled out, for his community, the accepted human pattern of authority. In his community, authority was to be *diakonia*, service. But what has been the christian record down the centuries, down to our day? Where power assumes paramount value, there lurks the ghost of Herod. Can we truthfully maintain that power is not still a cherished value of our ecclesiastical establishment? Let our christian *sisters* answer that one!

THE MAGI

The magi, mysterious people, are attractive people. They come, unexpectedly, out of the East, following their star. Their story that they had come seeking a new-born "king of the Jews" caused consternation in Jerusalem's political and ecclesiastical circles. Obviously, they were not regarded as cranks and were taken very seriously. Their openness and naivety must have impressed their worldly-wise hosts who could recognise such qualities—cynically aware that such virtues might be profitably exploited. The magi were fair game.

No doubt, they were made to feel welcome. They had no reason to suspect the counterfeit peity of Herod. After all, he was reigning king of the Jews; would he not, then, rejoice in the news that his successor promised to be a remarkable person? That would be good for Herod's people. No doubt, they had been flattered by a private audience. A touch of vanity is not reprehensible. For that matter, there is an innocent vanity that is a charming trait! Happily for them, these worthy men, like Joseph, were put straight.

The magi were romantic people: open-minded, and open-eyed to wonder; eager to follow a star; naive people, ready to believe the best of anybody. They were people "of whom the world was not worthy—wandering over deserts and mountains" (Heb 11:38). One can imagine the contempt of Herod and his courtiers for these innocents. Our world is a better place for such as they. We may have the good fortune to know their counterparts. More than ever, in our drab world, we need our starry-eyed dreamers—and more of them, please God!

ZECHARIAH AND ELIZABETH

"And they were both righteous before God, walking in all the commandments and ordinances of the Lord blameless" (Lk 1:6). A worthy Jewish couple, typical of the Anawim, the poor of the Lord. Despite their saintliness they carried the stigma of childlessness. They had learned to live with that but the pain is manifest in the words of an aged Elizabeth who thanked the good Lord for having "taken away her reproach among men" (Lk 1:25). At the close of their days they experienced unexpected joy; but it had been a long haul.

There are so many thoroughly good married people who have to live with pain. Not only with the loneliness of childlessness but with more bitter trials. A retarded child, or retarded children. The premature death or accident-injury of a child. The challenge of teen-age rebellon; the shock of drug-addiction. And, more recently, the challenge to their acceptance and sympathy of a son or daughter with Aids. The question cannot but arise: why should this happen to us? Virtuous living is no shield against suffering and tragedy. Zechariah and

Elizabeth were people of faith. They had come to terms with their situaton. They were open, too, to the utterly unexpected. They were those who were prepared to let God be God in *his* way. Because of that, Elizabeth was able to discern the action of God not only in her own case but in the person of Mary too. Trial had taught them humility and acceptance and had forged their fortitude. They needed fortitude, in their advanced years, to cope with a baby son.

THE SHEPHERDS

Jesus was no respecter of persons. That is a point ironically made in the fulsome flattery of opponents seeking to trap him: "We know that you are true, and care for no man; for you do not regard the position of men" (Mk 12:14). He was such because his God is no respecter of persons. Indeed, as the teaching and praxis of Jesus make clear, his God is a God with a preferential option for the poor and the marginalized. The Establishment could not have anticipated that the birth of the Messiah would first have been made known to those "who knew not the Law." They would not have hearkened to the testimony of such unlikely witnesses.

The shepherds are typical of the "simple faithful," very like the christian faithful of recent vintage whose role it was to "shut up and pay up." Since Vatican II the laity have been getting ideas—to the patent upset of some. Others would maintain that the only hope for the christian churches is that the ideas catch on, and quickly.

The shepherds are Luke's parallel to Matthew's magi and both groups play symbolic roles. The magi stand for a Gentile world, looking for salvation and open to the good news. The shepherds stand for those in Israel who did not have preconceived ideas about the way of salvation. Indeed, they may not have rated their own chances of salvation very highly; but they felt, deep down, like the tax collector of Jesus' parable, (Lk 18:9-14), that God could not really be as "the righteous" had painted him. Their native commonsense had sustaind their hope. Now these "simple" people take angelic message and heavenly glory in their stride and hurry to Bethlehem. They, too, are starry-eyed. And when they see a new-born babe in a manger they recognise, with an instinct uncomplicated by theology, that they are in the presence of God.

Luke has Jesus, in his Nazareth synagogue, proclaim the program of his mission: "to preach good news to the poor" (Lk 4:16-19). The same Luke, with this in mind, has taken care to have the birth of the Savior proclaimed first to the poor. Here, as in Matthew's magi story, our preoccupation with "historicity" is an intrusion. The shepherds are so utterly right in Luke's gospel, with his patent concern for the poor. And his shepherds do not keep the matter to themselves: they were the first preachers of the good news.

Here is a challenge to our official pattern of evangelization, a challenge to our western "efficiency." It may be that we have become too institutionalized—to the extent that we are, at least, uncomfortable at the thought that the Spirit may choose to operate outside approved channels. It seems to me that Luke and Matthew, each in his way, have made a similar point. Matthew has looked beyond a hostile Judaism to a receptive Gentile world. Luke has looked beyond a hostile Jewish establishment to a receptive "simple faithful." Marginalized Jew and Gentile "sinner" recognized and accepted what the Establishment had failed to recognize or had rejected. The infancy gospels underline the truth that the Gospel, because it is word of hope to "the poor" will always be word of threat to "the righteous.."

SIMEON

Simeon was a saintly, elderly man of strict religious obeservance who looked, with hope, to messianic deliverance. His hope was not misplaced because he was to receive heavenly assurance that before his death, he would meet the promised Messiah. He recognised that Messiah in the child brought by Mary and Joseph for presentation to the Lord in the Temple. He spoke prophetically of the child's saving role: a light of salvation for Gentiles as well as Israel—and a sign of contradiction. Dimly, Simeon had perceived the cross.

There is no suggestion that Simeon had any official place in the religious world of his day; he was the stolid lay-man. As one of the Anawim, he was faithful to temple cult and to times of prayer. He was able to rise above the inevitable formalism of cult and the abuses that marred the Temple precincts. It was house of God, and there he found his God. In his observance and in his prayer he was open to God and really heard the word of God.

Happily, there are still Simeons in our midst—many more, indeed, than we might think. They are not demonstrative people and do not get involved in controversy; they form no pressure group. Their peity is unobtrusive, but it is very real. They can live with sloppy liturgy and gimmicry because they can see beyond it. They can bear patiently and charitably with the foibles and failings of clergy. They can adapt to change. Though largely unnoticed, they form the backbone of a community. And the Holy Spirit works in them and through them.

ANNA

After a prophet a prophetess—the delicate hand of Luke. Anna is the counterpart of Simeon: she, too, a typical saint of Judaism, one of the Anawim. She, too, looked for "the redemption of Jerusalem." She is a faithful woman, anticipating the faithful women at the close of the gospel story. Her way of life illustrates the traditional piety and fortitude of women. But there is more to her than that. It is noteworthy that Anna not only recognised the new-born Messiah but "spoke of him to all who were looking for the redemption of Jerusalem." She exercized her "ministry of the word," again anticipating the ministerial role of women in the early Church.

It is all too easy to overlook this aspect of the portrait of Anna. She might seem to offer no more than a headline for an innocuous "order of widows" in 1 Tim 5:3-16. But, then, the Pastorals are already in reaction against woman ministry, or any authority role for women (cf. 1 Tim 2:11-15). Anna resembles Judith—she, too, a widow—a stalwart savior of Israel. In the story of Judith—the name means "the Jewess"— a downtrodden people gave expression, around the turn of the first century B.C., to its dream of deliverance; it is remarkable that the deliverer is a woman. Perhaps the intention is that deliverance would thereby stand out more starkly as achievement of God. Whether or not this is so, it must be that, by such a story, the honor of womankind is enhanced.

At the close of his gospel Luke tells us that the Galilean women disciples witnessed the burial of Jesus (23:55-56)— the men disciples had forsaken him (Mk 14:50). It was women who first heard the good news of resurrection (Lk 24:1-7). But when they proclaimed that good news "to the eleven and to all the rest," they met with disdain: "these words seemed to them an idle tale, and they did not believe them" (24:9-11), Luke has sketched an attitude that, sadly, was to grow and prevail. It is an attitude that is, rightly, being challenged in our day. An Anna who proclaimed Good News may offer hope to christian women.

THE BAPTIST

The role of prophet is never easy. The career of Jeremiah proves that abundantly. And Luke has Jeremiah in mind when announcing the birth of the Baptist. "He will be filled with the Holy Spirit, even from his mother's womb" (Lk 1:15) echoes "Before I formed you in the womb I knew you . . . I appointed you a prophet" (Jer 1:5). Jeremiah barely escaped death more than once; John was put to death. His glory will always be the accolade of the Lord: "I tell you, among those born of women none is greater than John" (Lk 7:28). Yet, the fact remains, Jesus did not walk the path of the Baptist. John was a prophet of doom. Jesus was a prophet of God's foolish love. Surely, not only in our day but in all days, we need the message of Jesus more than that of John.

For most of us Vatican II was a good thing. But there are those who look on it with a jaundiced eye and blame it for all our ills. There are those who maintain that, not Vatican II, but its aftermath, has been the breeding-ground of ill. And there are those—I among them—who discern, and regret, a concerted attempt to counteract something of that spirit of Vatican II. Perhaps this attempt is not too surprising in our day which is witnessing a widespread conservative turn. But it is to be regretted.

There is no escaping the fact that the demands of Jesus are radical. The contrast between Jesus and Baptist alerts us to the fact that a call to God's foolish love is far more challenging than a threat of God's "anger." Salutary warning is all very well: "You brood of vipers! Who warned you to flee from the wrath to come" (Lk 3:7). Dire threats like that may trigger a turn to repentance. So much more comforting and so much more challenging is the heartening assurance that God "rejoices more over one sinner who repents than over ninety-nine righteous persons who need no repentance" (Lk 15: 7, 10). And there is the scandalous conduct of the Father who welcomes and reinstates the prodigal without condition; the Father who throws a party for the sinner come home again (15:11-24). We have the assurance that the way of Jesus worked—and still works. It is fitting that a woman should be the one to give us the assurance. She is that anonymous woman in Luke 7, one who had encountered the loving Jesus and had received his gracious forgiveness. Her extravagant and "scandalous" response spoke so eloquently her joy. She had not been moved by warning or threat (and she had had plenty of both); she had been melted by goodness and sheer love.

The Baptist was the one who prepared the way of the Lord.

His task it was "to turn many . . . to the Lord their God" (1:16). It was his task, and he performed well. There is still need for his voice. But he can never have more than the first word. It is sad that, in christian tradition, the hell-fire preaching of the Baptist had tended to prevail. The institutional Church has, too often, found the Baptist more congenial than his Lord. If a pastor wants to go after the lost sheep, he likes to feel that the ninety-nine are safely corraled. Jesus is no help here—his word of unconditional forgiveness is subversive. It is not only the elder son who was scandalized by the foolish conduct of the Father (15:25-32). And there is the fact the the Baptist operated within a recognised and accepted structure, the structure of the Judaism of his day. The disturbing fact is that Jesus proclaimed a new, revolutionary, situation:

> The kings of the Gentiles exercize lordship over them; and those in authority over them are called benefactors. But not so with you; rather let the greatest among you become as the youngest, and the leader as one who serves (22:25-26).

It seems to me that this demand of the Lord, backed up by the example of his own life and death ("I am among you as one who serves," 22:27) has not been learned. There is much lip-service to *diakonia*. Let it be acknowledged, though, that, on the ground, there is more than lip-service. Yet, in the upper echelons, protestations of *diakonia* do not always ring true. The Baptist, true to his conviction, spoke out with courage and paid the price: he had challenged corruption in high places (Lk 3:19-20). Jesus had challenged the religious establishment—and paid the price (Lk 11:37-54). The Baptist and Jesus assure us that we will ever need our prophets. The Baptist and Jesus warn us that prophets never have been and never will be welcome in the realm of power. But then, power, especially ecclesiastical power, has always been a prime target of prophets.

MARY

If Mary has a low profile in Matthew's infancy gospel, she plays an important role in Luke. It is she, not Joseph, who is informed that her son will be of the Holy Spirit; it is she who will name her son. When she visits Elizabeth, she is hailed as a woman of faith. That visitation episode shows her as one recognisable in the Cana story of John (Jn 2:1-11). In Lk 1:39 Mary "went with haste" to Elizabeth's home. Hers was the resolute decision of a capable young woman who perceived a need and proceeded to do something about it. The Cana scene is heavy with symbolism. Yet, behind the veil of symbolism , appears a Mary who had been invited, as a practical woman, to organize a rural wedding. She was the first to notice an alarming shortage of wine—it could prove distressingly embarrassing for the bride and her family. Sensitive and warm-hearted, she discreetly drew attention to the predicament.

This picture of a level-headed, practical Mary is a necessary corrective to the traditional image of her. Her declaration—"I am the handmaid of the Lord"—has, through misunderstanding, not been helpful to the place of women in the Church. It has been used to establish them in a wholly passive role: how dare any woman aspire to anything more than Mary! There are a number of factors to be considered. The first is that of Semitic idiom. It was natural for a Jewish girl to describe herself, somewhat disparagingly, as "slave of the Lord." What matters is the Lord's assessment of her: the highly-favored one. Then there is the divine courtesy. God did not order Mary about: he courteously awaited her response. And, what is the difference between Mary's, "I am the handmaid of the Lord" and the statement: "the Son of man came not to be served but to serve" (Mk 10:45)? If he were Servant what wonder that she was Handmaid? It is necessary to challenge and set aside still prevalent images of Mary which diminish Mary and which limit the status and the role of women.

In this context it is not irrelevant to observe that the "Holy Family of Nazareth" has regularly, in Catholic piety, been presented as model of the christian family. It might seem such—at first sight; a closer look reveals it to be a less than helpful model. Virginal conception, angelic choirs, and a precocious twelve-year-old proclaiming himself Son of God, are not part of normal christian experience. A single-child family is not what most parents desire. And a life-long union without marital sex is not realistic, to put it mildly. The Holy Family is not the model of the christian family, nor was it ever meant to be. This is not to say, of course, that domestic virtues may not be sought and found there.

To return to Mary herself. It seems to me that Elizabeth's beatitude pinpoints what is most significantly helpful about Mary: "Blessed is she who believed" (Lk 1:45). She is the woman of faith. Popular piety has endowed her with extraordinary gifts. "Full of grace"—a mistranslation of the Greek phrase meaning "favored one"—gave *carte blanche*. It was assumed that she had been fully enlightened from the first as to the nature and destiny of her Son. So endowed was she thought to be indeed that she was hardly human any more. None of this is sustained by the gospel texts. In the gospels she appears very much one of us, as indeed she is. If her Son is like us in all things, the same must surely be true of the Mother. Nor does Mary's sinlessness make her any less human. Sin, whatever form it may take, detracts from our full humanness; it is a shadow on our humanness. Mary, as one wholly free of sin was wholly human. And being human necessarily involves the limitations of humanness. Sinlessness does not imply superhuman endowment; does not make one immune to suffering and to death.

There is one other point: Mary's *Magnificat*—which figures prominently in the liberation theology of Latin America. It is noteworthy that a woman, addressing a woman, emphasises God's preferential option for the poor. This woman speaks a subversive message. The traditional subservience of Mary must be challenged. The New Testament has little to say of her—but it says much more than has always been recognised. It is by acknowledging her whole and wholesome womanhood that she can be set free to help the cause of her sisters—not to be used against them.

JESUS

Our final look will be at the "star" of our stories—a star who plays a silent role. The Jesus of the infancy gospels is not, really, an anticipation of the Jesus of the ministry; instead, he reflects the Jesus of the ministry. The portrait of the baby is built out of what was known of his adult life. It was, rightly, discerned that what Jesus was seen to be during his ministry he had been from the very first. We may ask of the person and the role: what does he, himself, and what he stands for, mean for me here and now.

Happily for us the son of David is also son of Abraham—he is the Savior acknowledged by the magi. Yet, for thoughtful Gentile Christians, Israel's practical rejection of its Messiah must be very painful. It was certainly a problem for the first Christians. The prevalent view—as the christian movement became more and more non-Jewish—was that the "old Israel" had been replaced by a "new Israel." In my view, Paul will ever stand in protest against that solution. For him there could ever be only one Israel: a community of Jew *and* Gentile. God has surely *not* rejected his people (Rom 11:1-2). It seems to me that the positive theology of Matthew's genealogy is better than his later theology, colored as it is by bitter Jewish-Christian controversy (Mt 27:25; cf. Jn 19:12-15). There is need for Judeo-Christian dialogue. Our ecumenical endeavour cannot be confined to trying to patch together the splintered parts of Christianity; it must reach to linking with our roots. Again, I do believe that Paul has got it right (cf. Rom 11:17-24).

Jesus is Emmanuel—God-with-us. This is not quite the same as claiming that Jesus is God—a claim that may make sense or may involve serious christological distortion. It seems to me that the finest christological statement is that of Paul: "God was in Christ, reconciling the world to himself" (2 Cor 5:19). What a power of theology, and of soteriology, is there. Paul has told us where God is to be found: in Jesus of Nazareth, and why he is to be found in Jesus: to win humankind back to him. Where Jesus is, there is God. Logically, then, we have to find our God in a new-born babe, in a babe threatened by a paranoid king, in a baby who is a refugee, a displaced person. We are being challenged to see our God in one despised and rejected, in one tortured and hanging on a cross. A pious reading of the infancy gospels, leading to "a gentle Jesus, meek and mild," distorts the whole thrust of these stories. They are not " romantic" stories because they are shot-through with the cross. And, if one does not discern the cross, and the incredible love of God it speaks, one will never really know Emmanuel.

Is the Lucan picture less harsh? Not really. Of course; manger and swaddling cloths, so domestic; and angelic choir, so heavenly, provide an idyllic touch. The acclaim of shepherds is romantic. But there is the disturbing word—the sign of contradiction ; there is the sword piercing the soul of the mother. The shadow of the cross falls across this story too. There is no escaping it. It is not because our God is sadistic. It is because he is God of humankind, a God bent on the salvation of humankind. The suffering and death of Jesus confirm that suffering and death may be, and are, common experience of friends of God. Suffering and death—least of all the suffering and death of his own beloved Son—are not sought by God. Sadly, mysteriously, they *are* part of our human lot. Jesus—and the infancy gospels make plain that it was so from the beginning—was one who entered, wholly, into our human lot. In and through Jesus, God has assured us that he *is* the God "who did not spare his own Son" (Jn 3:16-17; Rom 5:6-11). Paul can rightly ask: "Will he not also give us all things with him?" (Rom 8:32).

I cannot, I simply cannot even begin to understand how Christians have perverted, as they have, the gracious purpose and deed of God. He has been made to seem a peevish God, waiting for due satisfaction. He has become victim of western logic and law. Happily, the real God, the Father of our Lord Jesus Christ, is the supremely free Hebrew God. We meet him in the exuberance and illogicality of the Christmas stories; we meet him in the supreme foolishness of the cross. Our western logic has ruined our Christmas story. Our western logic has nearly destroyed our God. Paul, that marvelous Hebrew, has pointed us to the truth: "for the foolishness of God is wiser than men, and the weakness of God is stronger than men" (1 Cor 1:25). We meet our God in a helpless and vulnerable babe—a savior trapped in swaddling clothes! We meet our God in one helplessly nailed to a cross! For me, at least, the evangelists have done a superb job. Each in his way, Matthew and Luke have, with brilliant imagination, brought back into their picture of babyhood and before, colors of the great saving drama. We speak, rightly, of infancy *gospels*. And, as in the gospels proper, there is no doubt as to who is the Star.

⥲ ❋ ⥱